ACTS

24 STUDIES FOR INDIVIDUALS AND GROUPS

N. T. WRIGHT

WITH DALE & SANDY LARSEN

IVP Connect

An imprint of InterVarsity Press
Downers Grove, Illinois

InterVarsity Press
P.O. Box 1400, Downers Grove, IL 60515-1426
World Wide Web: www.ivpress.com
E-mail: email@ivpress.com

This study guide is based on and includes excerpts adapted from Acts for Everyone: Part One *and* Acts for Everyone: Part Two, *©2008 Nicholas Thomas Wright. All Scripture quotations, unless otherwise indicated, are taken from the New Testament for Everyone. Copyright ©2001-2008 by Nicholas Thomas Wright. Used by permission of SPCK, London. All rights reserved.*

InterVarsity Press® *is the book-publishing division of InterVarsity Christian Fellowship/USA*®, *a movement of students and faculty active on campus at hundreds of universities, colleges and schools of nursing in the United States of America, and a member movement of the International Fellowship of Evangelical Students. For information about local and regional activities, write Public Relations Dept., InterVarsity Christian Fellowship/USA, 6400 Schroeder Rd., P.O. Box 7895, Madison, WI 53707-7895, or visit the IVCF website at <www.intervarsity.org>.*

Cover design: Cindy Kiple
Cover image: Michael Trevillion/Trevillion Images
Interior image: Clipart.com

ISBN 978-0-8308-2185-3

Printed in the United States of America ∞

P	19	18	17	16	15	14	13	12	11	10	9
Y	26	25	24	23	22	21	20	19	18	17	

CONTENTS

GETTING THE MOST OUT OF ACTS

The book of Acts is full of the energy and excitement of the early Christians as they found God doing new things all over the place and learned to take the good news of Jesus around the world. It's also full of the puzzles and problems that churches faced then and face today—crises over leadership, money, ethnic divisions, theology and ethics, not to mention serious clashes with political and religious authorities. It's comforting to know that "normal church life," even in the time of the first apostles, was neither trouble-free nor plain sailing, just as it's encouraging to know that even in the midst of all their difficulties the early church was able to take the gospel forward in such dynamic ways.

At one level, this book is the story of the early church—told very selectively, like all history, and told with an eye to particular concerns and interests. But Luke wants us to read it, all the way through, as a book about Jesus, a book indeed with Jesus as the principal actor, rather like some of the plays by Samuel Beckett, where the action on stage sometimes crucially depends on a person whom the audience never actually sees.

As a result, Luke wants us to read his work on another level as well. This is a play in which we are invited to become actors ourselves. The stage opens up and we discover we're in the middle of the action. That is part of the point of the "ending" which isn't really an ending: the story continues, and we are part of it.

As we do so, Luke is keen that we latch on to two things which are fundamental to his whole book and his whole view of the world. First, everything is based on the resurrection of Jesus. In the last chapter of his Gospel, Luke described some of the scenes in which Jesus met his followers after being raised from the dead: he was really alive, richly alive, in a transformed body that could eat and drink as well as walk and talk but which seemed to have . . . some different properties. His body could, for instance, appear and disappear, and come and go through locked doors.

To us, that sounds as if he was a ghost, someone less than properly embodied. What Luke and the other writers who describe the risen body of Jesus are saying, rather, is that Jesus is *more* than ordinarily embodied, not less. His transformed body is the beginning of God's new creation in which heaven and earth will come together in a new way (Revelation 21 and Ephesians 1). Jesus' risen body is the beginning of a heavenly reality which is fully at home on, and in, this physical world, and the beginning of a transformed physical world which is fully at home in God's sphere. The point of the resurrection itself is that without it there is no gospel, no ongoing work of Jesus. There would only be the sad memory of a great but failed teacher and would-be Messiah. The resurrection of Jesus who died under the weight of the world's evil is the foundation of the new world, God's new world, whose opening scenes Luke is describing.

The second thing Luke wants us to latch onto, which he gets to right at the beginning, is the presence and power of the Holy Spirit. From the start he insists that the Spirit is present and that they are about to discover the Spirit as a new and powerful reality in the lives of his followers. Rather than being John's baptism of water and repentance to restore Israel, the Spirit's baptism would restore humanity, celebrating the fact that God was becoming king of the whole world, and knowing that as a reality inside their own selves. At the heart of Luke's book is that God is at work doing a new thing in the whole world. (For more on this book, also see my *Acts for Everyone: Part One* and *Acts for Everyone: Part Two*, published by SPCK and Westminster John Knox. This guide is based on those books and was prepared with the help of Dale and Sandy Larsen, for which I am grateful.)

Acts is a book where more journeys take place than anywhere else in the Bible—with the last journey, in particular, including a terrific storm and a dramatic shipwreck. There isn't a dull page in the story. But equally important, the whole book reminds us, as I said earlier, that we are part of the story ourselves. Whatever "journey" we are making, in our own lives, our spirituality, our following of Jesus, and our work for his kingdom, his Spirit will guide us too, and make us fruitful in his service.

SUGGESTIONS FOR INDIVIDUAL STUDY

1. As you begin each study, pray that God will speak to you through his Word.

2. Read the introduction to the study and respond to the "Open" question that follows it. This is designed to help you get into the theme of the study.

3. Read and reread the Bible passage to be studied. Each study is designed to help you consider the meaning of the passage in its context. The commentary and questions in this guide are based on my own translation of each passage found in the companion volume to this guide in the For Everyone series on the New Testament (published by SPCK and Westminster John Knox).

4. Write your answers to the questions in the spaces provided or in a personal journal. Each study includes three types of questions: observation questions, which ask about the basic facts in the passage; interpretation questions, which delve into the meaning of the passage; and application questions, which help you discover the implications of the text for growing in Christ. Writing out your responses can bring clarity and deeper understanding of yourself and of God's Word.

5. Each session features selected comments from the For Everyone series. These notes provide further biblical and cultural background and contextual information. They are designed not to answer the questions for you but to help you along as you study the Bible for

yourself. For even more reflections on each passage, you may wish to have on hand a copy of the companion volume from the For Everyone series as you work through this study guide.

6. Use the guidelines in the "Pray" section to focus on God, thanking him for what you have learned and praying about the applications that have come to mind.

SUGGESTIONS FOR GROUP MEMBERS

1. Come to the study prepared. Follow the suggestions for individual study mentioned above. You will find that careful preparation will greatly enrich your time spent in group discussion.

2. Be willing to participate in the discussion. The leader of your group will not be lecturing. Instead, she or he will be asking the questions found in this guide and encouraging the members of the group to discuss what they have learned.

3. Stick to the topic being discussed. These studies focus on a particular passage of Scripture. Only rarely should you refer to other portions of the Bible or outside sources. This allows for everyone to participate on equal ground and for in-depth study.

4. Be sensitive to the other members of the group. Listen attentively when they describe what they have learned. You may be surprised by their insights! Each question assumes a variety of answers. Many questions do not have "right" answers, particularly questions that aim at meaning or application. Instead the questions push us to explore the passage more thoroughly.

    When possible, link what you say to the comments of others. Also, be affirming whenever you can. This will encourage some of the more hesitant members of the group to participate.

5. Be careful not to dominate the discussion. We are sometimes so eager to express our thoughts that we leave too little opportunity for others to respond. By all means participate! But allow others to also.

6. Expect God to teach you through the passage being discussed and through the other members of the group. Pray that you will have an enjoyable and profitable time together, but also that as a result of the study you will find ways that you can take action individually and/ or as a group.

7. It will be helpful for groups to follow a few basic guidelines. These guidelines, which you may wish to adapt to your situation, should be read at the beginning of the first session.

   • Anything said in the group is considered confidential and will not be discussed outside the group unless specific permission is given to do so.

   • We will provide time for each person present to talk if he or she feels comfortable doing so.

   • We will talk about ourselves and our own situations, avoiding conversation about other people.

   • We will listen attentively to each other.

   • We will be very cautious about giving advice.

Additional suggestions for the group leader can be found at the back of the guide.

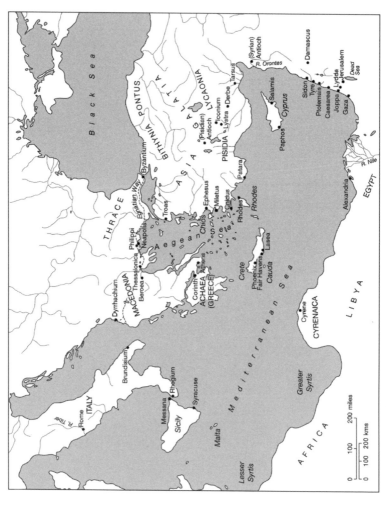

The Eastern Mediterranean in the first century A.D.

LUKE'S STORY CONTINUES

Acts 1

The opening paragraph of the book of Acts declares, clearly and solidly, that it is a sequel. There has been a previous book, and this one continues the story. It even suggests a kind of title: *The Deeds and Teachings of King Jesus, Part Two*. At first sight this is a strange title, since Jesus himself only appears during the first nine verses of the first chapter. But Luke, whose first volume we know as the Gospel which bears his name, is telling us in his opening sentence one of the most important things about this second book. It is all about what Jesus is continuing to do and to teach.

The mysterious presence of Jesus haunts the whole story. He is announced as King and Lord, not as an increasingly distant memory but as a living and powerful reality, a person who can be known and loved, obeyed and followed, a person who continues to act within the real world. We call the book "The Acts of the Apostles," but we should think of it as "The Acts of Jesus (II)."

OPEN

How do you respond to the idea that Jesus is "a person who can be known and loved, obeyed and followed, a person who continues to act within the real world"?

STUDY

1. *Read Acts 1:1-14.* For what are the apostles eager and even impatient?

2. How does Jesus deal with their eagerness and impatience?

3. Think of a time when you were eager to get started with something, and you had to wait. What was the value of waiting?

Jesus' motley band of followers had imagined that he would be king in some quite ordinary sense, which was why some of them had asked if they could have the top jobs in his government. Jesus, with his extraordinary healing power and visionary teaching, would rule in Jerusalem and would restore God's people Israel. Israel would be the top nation, ruling over the rest of the world.

In the resurrection (and the ascension described in vv. 9-10), Jesus is indeed being enthroned as Israel's Messiah and therefore king of the whole world. The apostles must go out as heralds, not of someone who may become king at some point in the future, but of the one who has already been appointed and enthroned.

4. Picture yourself as one of the apostles at the ascension (vv. 9-11). What do you see and hear?

5. Still picturing yourself at Jesus' ascension, how do you react to the experience? What do you think, feel, say and do?

In the Bible, heaven is not a location within our own cosmos of space, time and matter. Heaven and earth are the two halves of God's created reality. *Heaven* is God's dimension, and *earth* is ours. From the ascension onward, the story of Jesus' followers takes place in both dimensions. Heaven may well be our temporary home after this present life; but the whole new heaven-and-earth combination, united and transformed, is our eventual destination (see Revelation 21:1-4). The risen body of Jesus is the first, and so far the only, object which is fully at home in both spheres, anticipating the time when everything will be renewed and joined together. Jesus has gone into God's dimension of reality; but he will be back on the day when that dimension and our present one are brought together once and for all. That promise hangs in the air over the whole of Christian history from that day to this. That is what we mean by the *second coming*.

6. The apostles and others in the young church all gave themselves single-heartedly to prayer (v. 14). What do you think drove them to intense prayer at this time?

7. What has driven (or still drives) you to a time of intense prayer?

8. How does the urgent need for prayer affect your relationship with Christ?

All those who name the name of Jesus, who worship him, who study his Word, are called to be people of worship and prayer. It is precisely in worship and prayer that we, while still on "earth" in the sense I've suggested already, find ourselves sharing the life of "heaven," which is where Jesus is. (For a fuller discussion of heaven see my book *Surprised by Hope*.)

9. *Read Acts 1:15-26.* What attitudes and responses do the disciples have toward Judas's death?

10. What resources do the young church turn to for the solution to the problem of how to replace Judas?

11. What approach and resources does your church or fellowship usually take to solve a problem?

12. What do you learn from how your approach compares with the approach the apostles took?

13. Luke's Gospel is his account of the life of Jesus. Acts is the continuing story of Jesus' ministry. How do you see the continuing ministry of Jesus in your own life?

PRAY

Consider what you think the first Christians prayed for in the upstairs room (Acts 1:13-14) and pray your own similar prayers.

NOTE ON ACTS 1:9-10

Luke tells us that Jesus was "lifted up" or "taken up." This does not indicate that he was heading out somewhere beyond the moon or Mars, but that he was going into God's dimension. The cloud, as is so often the case in the Bible, is the sign of God's presence. That's how the disciples would have understood it. Think of the pillar of cloud and fire as the children of Israel wandered through the desert (Exodus 14:19-24), or the cloud and smoke that filled the temple when God became suddenly present in a new way (2 Chronicles 5:14).

First-century readers would also have picked up a reference to Daniel 7, where "one like a son of man" is brought up, on the clouds of heaven, to the "Ancient of Days," and is presented before him and given kingly power over the nations. The story of Jesus' ascension would indicate that Daniel 7 had been fulfilled in a dramatic and unexpected way. This clearly contrasts with verses 6-8 and their discussion of the wrong kind of kingly enthronement the disciples imagined.

Wind and Fire

Acts 2:1-41

All Christians, not only those who call themselves Pentecostalists, derive their meaning from the first Pentecost. For a first-century Jew, Pentecost was the fiftieth day after Passover. It was an agricultural festival. But Passover and Pentecost also awakened echoes of the great story of the exodus from Egypt, when the people of Israel crossed the Red Sea and God rescued his people from slavery. Fifty days after Passover, the Israelites came to Mount Sinai, where Moses received the law. Pentecost is about God giving to his redeemed people the way of life by which they must now carry out his purposes. Now Jesus has gone up into heaven in the ascension, and he is now coming down again, not with a written law carved on tablets of stone, but with the dynamic energy of the law, designed to be written on human hearts.

OPEN

What comes to your mind when the Holy Spirit is mentioned?

STUDY

1. *Read Acts 2:1-13.* "They" (v. 1) are apparently the same group of 120 or so identified in Acts 1:15. What evidences are presented here of the Holy Spirit in action?

2. What is the significance of people from all over the Mediterranean region hearing the disciples speak each in their own native languages?

3. What has the Spirit done in our midst recently that has grabbed the attention of others? If nothing, why is that so?

It is most significant, in the light of the ascension, that the wind came "from heaven" (2:2). The whole point is that, through the Spirit, some of the creative power of God himself comes from heaven to earth and does its work there. The aim is not to give people a "spirituality" which will make the things of earth irrelevant. The point is to transform earth with the power of heaven, starting with those parts of "earth" which consist of the bodies, minds, hearts and lives of the followers of Jesus.

The coming of the Spirit at Pentecost is the complementary fact to the ascension of Jesus into heaven. The risen Jesus in heaven is the presence, in God's sphere, of the first part of "earth" to be transformed into "new creation." In Jesus heaven and earth are thus joined. The pouring out of the Spirit on earth is the presence, in our sphere, of the heaven itself. The gift of the Spirit is thus the direct result of the ascension of Jesus.

4. The Jews of the first century read their Scriptures as saying that their generation was the one for which prophecy would come true. They were eager for signs that Israel had at last arrived at their destination and God was bringing about the fulfillment of his promises.

   Read Acts 2:14-21. How does Peter use Joel's prophecy (found in Joel 2:28-32) to explain what was happening?

5. Previously, in the Old Testament, God had acted by his Spirit through one or two key people at a time. How is this action of God's Spirit new?

6. What should be the significance of this widespread action of the Spirit for how our church or fellowship carries out its work?

   Israel expected God to act in a powerful way to set his people free; but the language they would use for cataclysmic events like that was the language of what we call "cosmic" events. So it wouldn't surprise Peter's audience that he should mention fire and clouds of smoke, and the sun being turned to darkness and the moon into blood. All of nature would be affected, and his listeners could easily imagine or recall a great eclipse or other natural phenomena. For the prophets, these were regular ways of referring to "earth-shattering events"—changes in society and global politics that would shake the foundations of our world.

7. Read Acts 2:22-41. Peter quotes Psalm 16 in Acts 2:25-28, saying it is a prophecy about Jesus. Even though David wrote the psalm, what evidence does Peter give that David can't possibly be talking about himself here?

8. Why does Peter say the psalm must be talking about Jesus instead?

9. Peter then quotes Psalm 110 in Acts 2:34-35. How does this add to his argument that Jesus is Israel's true Lord?

10. How do Peter's hearers respond to his words that they had crucified the one God made Lord and Messiah?

This is perhaps the first beginning, the first small glimpse, of the church's developing understanding of the cross. That understanding doesn't begin as an abstract theory about sin or judgment. It begins as the very concrete and specific awareness: "this corrupt generation" is heading for disaster, but Jesus stands in the way and can stop them from falling over the cliff. The message is clear: "Be rescued!" You need to turn back, to repent. You need to be baptized, to join the company marked out with the sign of the new exodus, coming through the water to leave behind slavery and sin and to find the way to freedom and life.

In this passage we are witnessing the beginning of the Christian theme called *salvation*. "Salvation" points toward a very concrete and particular reality in the future, the promise not only of heaven after death but of resurrection into God's new creation. What God has promised for the ultimate future has come forward to meet us in Jesus Christ. Whenever we are in a mess, of whatever sort and for whatever reason, we should remember that we are "turn-back-and-be-rescued" people. We are "repent-and-be-baptized" people.

11. When and how did you first respond to the urgent message to "let God rescue you"?

12. What does it mean for us this week that we are "turn-back-and-be-rescued" people?

PRAY

Thank God for the gift of his Holy Spirit, and for the promise of the new creation both now and in the future. Bring to God anything and everything from which you need to be rescued right now: physical and spiritual threats, persistent sins, wrong attitudes, relationships which seem beyond repair, seemingly impossible situations. Praise him in advance for his answers.

NOTE ON ACTS 2:17-21

Jews of Peter's day saw themselves as the generation when God's promises to Israel would be fulfilled. The book of Daniel was most carefully studied in the first century, and people knew they were living about 490 years after the Babylonian exile, the very timeframe discussed in Daniel 9:24. At the same time they studied, memorized, prayed over and puzzled over many other old texts, texts which spoke of terrible things that would happen but of a time when it would all be reversed, when God would bring them to a new place and do quite new things with them. And some of the texts spoke of the signs that they would see when they arrived at that moment, the signals that would say, "You're here! This is where you were going!"

It's only by imagining that world that we can understand how Peter could even think of launching in to a great long quotation from the prophet Joel in order to explain the apparently confused babbling and shouting that was going on. Yes, Peter says, this must be a sign that these are indeed "the last days."

What did "the last days" mean? It was a general term in the first century for the time to come, the time when promises would be fulfilled and the story of God and Israel would arrive at its climax. While Peter declares that these are "the last days," it is not "the last day" itself. There remains another "day" (not necessarily a period of twenty-four hours, but a moment or coming time) which the prophets referred to as "the day of the Lord." But now they understood "Lord" to refer to Jesus. The early Christians believed, in other words, that they were living in a period of time between the moment when "the last days" had been launched and the moment when even those "last days" would come to an end on "the day of the Lord," the moment when, with Jesus' final reappearance (already promised in Acts 1:11), heaven and earth would be joined together in the great coming renewal of all things (see Acts 3:21 and Revelation 21:1-4).

RESTORATION AND REFRESHMENT

Acts 2:42–3:26

Again and again, in worship and sacrament, in reading the Scriptures, in Christian fellowship and prayer, we taste in advance just a little bit of the coming together of heaven and earth, the sense that this is what we were made for, the new world which we shall finally enjoy. It is there, available, ready for all who seriously seek it. Believing in Jesus and in the power of his name is the way to wholeness, in the twenty-first century just as in the first.

OPEN

When have you felt refreshed physically or spiritually? Describe what it was like.

STUDY

1. *Read Acts 2:42-47.* Imagine a world without any Christian church. If you lived in such a world, and then suddenly found yourself swept

up in this pattern of teaching, fellowship, bread-breaking and prayer, what would be your reaction?

2. Acts 2:42 is often regarded as laying down the "four marks of the church": the apostles' teaching; the common life of those who believed; the breaking of bread; and the prayers. These four go together. You can't separate them or leave one out without damage to the whole thing.

    Look at each of the four. What risks does a church face if any one of these is absent or neglected?

3. Which of these four is weakest in your Christian community, and how might it be strengthened?

4. How else did the early Christians express their common life in practical ways (2:43-47)?

5. These early believers seem not to have sold the houses in which they lived, since they went on meeting in individual homes (2:46). Rather, they sold extra property they possessed—a highly significant thing for people for whom land was not just an economic asset but part of their ancestral heritage, part of God's promised inheritance.

    Christians saw themselves as a single family. Just as a biological family would share shelter, food and money, so did the early Christians. They also shared more of course—the same baptism, faith and fellowship.

In what ways can we express this common life and bond that we have with other Christians, materially and otherwise?

6. *Read Acts 3:1-16.* In what ways is the encounter Peter and John have with the lame man what would be expected? And how would it be unexpected?

7. What is the significance of Peter's words "In the name of the Messiah, Jesus of Nazareth" (3:6)?

Up to now, in Acts, the whole story has taken place in Jerusalem, but not in or around the temple. Now the demonstration of the power of Jesus' name took place not in the temple, but outside the gate. God is on the move, not confined within the power structure of an institution. Luke's Gospel began and ended in the temple. But now he is telling us that the good news of Jesus is starting to reach outside to anyone and everyone who needs it.

8. Jesus had taught great crowds at the temple only a few weeks before, and he had then been crucified. Now Peter and John are attracting major attention in the temple (3:11).

What's the significance of each thing Peter has to say about Jesus in 3:13-16?

9. In Acts 3:16 Peter says the man was healed in Jesus' name, yes; but it was not just a magical incantation. What more was involved and what does that mean?

10. *Read Acts 3:17-26.* What are the results of repentance (3:19-20)?

11. How have you seen those results in your own life?

12. In Acts 3:21-26, how, according to Peter, do Moses and the prophets point to Jesus?

There is coming a time when God will restore all things. And though that final day will be truly wonderful, it can be anticipated with times of refreshment in the present. Like so much early Christian belief, this is basically a Jewish belief about the future, based on the solid rock of belief in God as both creator and judge, but rethought now around the events concerning Jesus. The ultimate promise of verse 21 is firmly rooted in the Jewish prophets. What has changed now is that the final restoration has already happened to Jesus himself. What God is going to do to the whole of creation, he has done for Jesus in raising him from the dead.

13. How do you long to be refreshed right now?

PRAY

Thank God for forgiveness of sins. Pray for yourself, that you will be restored, healed and refreshed in every way. Pray the same for others who are in need physically and spiritually.

NOTE ON ACTS 3:14-17

Tragically, Christians have sometimes taken passages like this and suggested that they mean that the Jewish people were somehow always to be blamed for what had happened to Jesus. The reverse is the case. Not only is there no sense, in Acts or elsewhere, that the Jewish people somehow bear guilt or blame beyond the initial people who rejected Jesus himself. There is, on the contrary, the extended invitation, rooted in God's covenant faithfulness, for them to receive forgiveness and refreshment as much as anyone else. The promise of the restoration of all things is, after all, a deeply Jewish promise. None of the first Christians, who were of course all themselves Jewish, would have imagined that God would turn his back on the very people who had carried that promise through so many generations.

4

CLASH OF LOYALTIES

Acts 4:1-31

What was it about the early Christian message which got the authorities, and others too, so alarmed and angry? Wouldn't it be simply great *Jesus rose from the dead* news to know that God was alive and well and was providing a wonderful rescue operation through his chosen Messiah?

Answer: not if you were already in power. Not if you were one of the people who had rejected and condemned that Messiah. And not, particularly, if you were in charge of the central institution that administered God's law, God's justice and the life of God's people, and you strongly suspected that this new movement was trying to upstage you, to diminish or overturn that power and prestige and take it for itself.

OPEN

In what situations do you find yourself praying most easily? Explain.

STUDY

1. *Read Acts 4:1-22.* The Sadducees were Jewish aristocrats, including the high priest and his family, who for some years had wielded great

power in Jerusalem and among the Jewish people generally. That is
why they strongly disapproved of the idea of resurrection. Resurrection was a radical, dangerous doctrine. If God is going to suddenly
put everything right once and for all, they cannot guarantee that they
will end up in power in the new world that God is going to make.

What do the religious leaders want to know about the healing described in Acts 3:1-10?

2. What does Peter make most prominent in his defense?
God of Abraham + God fulfilled his prophecy.

3. What strikes you as the boldest part of Peter's defense?
Saying they crucified Christ, they must believe to have salvation

Acts 4:12 has been unpopular within the politically correct climate
of the last few generations in the Western world. "No other name"?
People say this is arrogant or exclusive; and so it can be if Christians
use the name of Jesus to further their own power or prestige. But for
many years now the boot has been on the other foot. It is the secu-
larists and the relativists who have acted the part of the chief priests,
protecting their cherished temple of modernist thought. They claim
to know exclusively what should and should not be believed.

4. What "names" do people call on today in hopes that they will be
rescued from their problems?

5. How can we constructively respond to these viewpoints?

6. How do the authorities know that Peter and John were people who "had been with Jesus" (v. 13)? *H ealed a man* .

7. What do the authorities ask Peter and John, and how does Peter respond? *Not too teach about Jesus & Peter said they should obey God not man*

8. In what situations, for you or others, have you known of tensions between listening to God and listening to human authorities? Describe them and what happened.

9. How are Christians to show respect both for human authorities and God's authority?

Book learning is often a poor substitute for firsthand experience if you really want to get inside a subject or have it inside you. That was what was so striking about Peter and John. Clearly they hadn't been to rabbinical school to study the Scriptures. They had a secret— a secret that enabled them to run rings around the book learning of the authorities. They had been with Jesus. This didn't just give them boldness in the sense of courage to stand up and say what they thought. It gave them something more: a clarity, a sharp edge, a definite point at which to stand.

10. *Read Acts 4:23-31.* Those who gather after Peter and John are released pray from Psalm 2, a text which stands within a long Jewish tradition in which God places his chosen people amidst the warring and violent nations of the earth as a sign of his coming kingdom. All this

will come through the Messiah as the Son of God, by whose rule he will eventually bring peace and justice to the world.

How does this Scripture passage set a context that helps these early Christians understand and deal with their own situation?

11. The church did not pray "Lord, let this persecution stop," or "Please convert the authorities so that your work can go forward." Rather, quite simply, they prayed "Now, Lord, look on their threats; let us go on speaking boldly; and will you please continue to work powerfully." The opposition are there, and God knows about them. We are here, and we need to be faithful, to continue to speak of Jesus boldly and confidently. And here is the power of God, which is not in our possession but which, because of Jesus, will continue to be at work to set up signposts pointing people to the new thing which is happening through him.

Who or what is opposing your witness or your church's witness for Christ? *Politics , Self,*

12. How have you been praying so far about the opposition, and how might your prayers now change? *That I can understand their side*

PRAY

Using the young church's prayer (Acts 4:24-30) as your example, pray about opposition to the gospel message, both in your own area and throughout the world.

5

THE NEW COMMUNITY

Acts 4:32–5:42

Luke has already introduced several themes which will be important as his book progresses. Next he emphasizes the way in which the early church was living as the true people of God—not least, we may suspect, in order to highlight an emerging paradox. The temple authorities thought *they* were the guardians of the official traditions of Israel; but, in the very same city, there was a community which was practicing the life of the true covenant people of God and thereby quietly upstaging all that went on in the temple.

What you do with money and possessions declares loudly what sort of a community you are, and the statement made by the early church's practice was clear and definite. No wonder they were able to give such powerful testimony to the resurrection of Jesus. They were demonstrating that it was a reality in ways that many Christians today, who often sadly balk at even giving a tithe of their income to the church, can only dream of.

OPEN

Describe when you've experienced a sense of community.

STUDY

1. *Read Acts 4:32–5:11.* Describe the way the believers lived (4:32-35).

2. How do you react to the events of Acts 4:36–5:11?

3. Why do you think there was such severe judgment against Ananias and Sapphira?

4. What happens today when there is dishonesty among Christians?

5. In what areas of life are we (or are we at least tempted to be) less than honest?

Luke is telling us that the early Christian community was functioning somewhat like the temple itself. It was a place of holiness, a holiness so dramatic and acute that every blemish was magnified. If you want to be a community which seems to be taking the place of the temple of the living God, you mustn't be surprised if the living God takes you seriously, seriously enough to make it clear that there is no such thing as cheap grace. If you invoke the power of the Holy One, the one who will eventually right all wrongs, and sort out all cheating and lying, he may just decide to do some of that work already, in advance (though this never seems to happen again in the early church, with the possible exception of 1 Corinthians 11:30 and the warning of 1 Corinthians 5:1-5). We either choose to live in the presence of the God who made the world and who longs passionately for it to be set right, or we lapse back into some variety of easy-going paganism, even if it has a Christian veneer. Holiness is not an optional extra. To name the name of Jesus and to invoke the Holy Spirit is to claim to be the temple of the living God, and that is bound to have consequences.

6. *Read Acts 5:12-42.* We would expect anyone to welcome the wonderful things described in verses 12-16. How and why do the high priest and the Sadducees react to what was happening (5:17-28)?

7. How does God vindicate the apostles?

8. One of the fascinating things about Acts is that no one knew what to call the new movement. Not until chapter 11 will the followers of Jesus be called *Christians.* There is a bewildering variety of names and descriptions given not just to the apostles and their larger company but to the movement itself. Here in verse 5:20, for the only time, it is referred to as *this Life.*

   Why is "this Life" or "this new life" an appropriate designation for faith in Jesus Christ?

9. The angel told the apostles to go take their stand in the temple and speak (5:20). Wordless symbols, however powerful, remain open to a variety of explanations. From the very beginning, the apostolic faith has been something that demands to be explained, that needs to be taught. Without words to guide it, faith wanders in the dark and can easily fall over a cliff. We will see in the next chapter that speaking was one of the two primary tasks to which the apostles were called, the other being prayer.

When have you found the need to explain your faith?

10. How do the apostles respond to what the Jewish leaders did and said?

11. Is Gamaliel's analysis and counsel in 5:33-39 correct or not? Explain.

12. The church can never anticipate who will suddenly speak up for our right to exist and to preach and teach about Jesus. Our job is to be faithful and, when a clash comes, to obey God rather than human authorities.

    What would such faithfulness look like for you and your Christian community?

13. The apostles rejoiced that they were found worthy to suffer for Jesus' name. How could it be an honor for them (and us) to be dishonored?

PRAY

Pray that you will live in honesty before God and before others, whether believers or unbelievers. Thank God for sending people to intervene on your behalf when it was needed. Pray that God will give you the privilege of being the right person in the right place at the right time for someone else.

THE FAMILY WIDENS

Acts 6

Already in the early days, Jesus' followers faced problems about how to run things. From the beginning they had shared their resources, a sign that they knew they were called to live as a single family. But how is that going to work when the family is suddenly double the size you expected it to be? You're going to have to sort something out pretty quickly. The pressure in the early movement came to a head along the fault line which would continue to be a problem for many years to come: the distinctions between people from different ethnic and linguistic groupings and the question of their relative status within the new movement. Whenever a small number of people try to live together, let alone share resources, sometimes even tiny distinctions of background and culture can loom very large and have serious consequences.

OPEN

What differences have you appreciated about Christians from a background very different from yours, and why do you appreciate them?

STUDY

1. *Read Acts 6:1-15.* What is the dispute among the believers (vv. 1-2)?

   The Greek widows didn't recieve daily food

2. How do the apostles deal with the dispute (vv. 2-6)?

   They chose 7 men full of the Spirit + wisdom to decide what to do,

3. Why don't the apostles take over the matter themselves?

   They wanted to use their attention on prayer + ministry of the word

4. The seven men chosen (later called *deacons,* meaning *servants*) were "well spoken of and filled with the Spirit and wisdom" (v. 3). In addition, Stephen was a man full of faith and the Holy Spirit (v. 5). Those qualities sound more "spiritual" than practical. Why are those qualities needed in ministering to people of varied backgrounds where there is tension and jealousy? *the spiritual They need God's ability to make wise decision + the*

5. Jerusalem was both a deeply traditional culture and a cosmopolitan mixture of Jews from all over the world. Native-born Palestinian Jews, who spoke Aramaic as their mother tongue, would feel they had more in common with one another than with the Greek-speaking folk who had come from the wider world. The "Hebrews" or "Hebraic Jews" mentioned in verse 1 referred to the early Christians from this first group. The "Hellenists" or "Grecian Jews" were Christians from the second group who had returned to Jerusalem after years or perhaps generations away.

Where are the dividing lines of tension and jealousy among Christians in your own fellowship? *financial — where is the best place to spend money, We must be careful with politics new + old members —*

6. Taking Acts 6:1-6 as your example, what are some possible ways to bridge the divisions in your own fellowship? *Realize we aren't always in agreement but that we all may have valid points.*

7. How does the young church apparently benefit from the solution which God gave the apostles? *Remember if our backgrounds are different to be excepting of everybody*

8. Stephen was one of the seven chosen to take care of the food distribution (v. 5). He was apparently at home in the wider world of Greek-speaking Jews. What other work also occupied him (vv. 8-10)? *He did great wonders + miraculous signs among the people.*

9. What do Stephen's enemies accuse him of (vv. 9-14)? *Speaking against Moses + speaking about Jesus.*

10. Why are they frustrated, and what do they do about it? *They saw he looked like an angel —*

Seen from the point of view of a hard-line first-century Jew, there is a grain of truth in at least two of the accusations against Stephen, that he was undermining the law of Moses and speaking against the temple. But in actuality the early Christian claim was that the God of our ancestors, in fulfillment of the purposes for which he gave the law and the temple in the first place, was now doing a new thing. God really did give the law and the temple, but this was part of a great story which has now reached a new point.

11. As he listened to the accusations, Stephen's face "was like the face of an angel" (v. 15). Since as far as we know neither the assembly nor Luke had ever seen an angel, what is the phrase meant to communicate?

    He looked like he had the peace of God in him.

12. How did Stephen's qualifications for being a deacon equip him to face persecution?

    He was wise + full of the holy spirit.

13. What will equip you to face distorted accusations? Explain.

    Knowing God is with me,

PRAY

Pray for God's solution to divisions in your church fellowship. Pray for the right people to come forward to take action. Before God, assess your own willingness to be one of those people.

7

STEPHEN TELLS THE STORY

Acts 7:1–8:3

One of the great arts of Christian theology is to know how to tell the story: the story of the Old Testament, the story of Jesus as both the climax of the Old Testament and the foundation of all that was to come (not a random collection of useful preaching material with some extraordinary and saving events tacked on the end), and the story of the church from the first days until now. Sometimes a story is the only way of telling the truth. In this Scripture we see Stephen telling the story to an unfriendly audience under life-and-death circumstances.

OPEN

When has a story—a book, a movie, an account you heard—upset you, and why?

STUDY

1. Stephen has been called before the Jewish elders, scribes and high priest, accused of speaking against four holy centers of Israel's

faith—God, Moses, the temple and the law (see 6:11, 13-14). *Read Acts 7:1-16.* Stephen could have waved the charges away as obviously false, or he could have avoided them and used the opportunity to speak about Jesus himself. What does he begin to do instead?

2. What high points in the story of the Jewish people does Stephen bring out in 7:1-16?

Much of Stephen's speech does not seem to be a direct answer to the charges made against him. Instead of a head-on rebuttal of the charges, he has chosen a kind of outflanking movement. Tell the story *this* way, he is saying, and you will see what I am saying about Jesus and how it relates to everything else that matters. Stephen starts with Abraham because it is with Abraham that the story of the Jewish people begins; and it is with Abraham that Genesis begins the story of *how the world is to be set right.*

3. Stephen has been accused of going soft on Moses and his law; very well, he will go back to the story of Moses and see what it says. *Read Acts 7:17-53.* What main points of Moses' life does Stephen choose to emphasize?

4. How does Stephen suggest in his retelling that it wasn't him who rejected Moses but the ancestors of the Jews who actually rejected him?

5. The question of the Holy Land looms large in Stephen's speech even though it's not been mentioned in the charges laid against him. Glance through Acts 7:1-53. Which geographical areas are emphasized (and which are not) in Stephen's story of God's work in the people of Israel?

6. Why would this have upset his accusers?

7. Having dealt with Moses and the question of what is really holy land at length, Stephen quickly discusses the temple in particular in 7:44-50. What challenges does he bring to the way the Jews would have understood the central role and significance of the temple for Israel?

8. Stephen's speech suddenly stops being a careful historical account of the early days of Israelite history and draws swiftly and shockingly to its close in a burst of denunciation. Of what does Stephen specifically accuse them in 7:51-53?

9. In particular how are they similar in this way to their ancestors in the portrait he has painted in this chapter?

Wherever God reveals himself as the savior of his people, bringing about plans which, though they seem new and surprising, are nev-

ertheless the fulfillment of what he had said long ago, that place becomes holy. Stephen is saying that the holiness of what God has done
and is doing in Jesus himself is now substantially upstaging the holiness of their own homemade, handmade system and building.

10. As we consider our own traditions and think of them lovingly since
they "prove" that we are in the right place in our worship and witness, perhaps sometimes we need to allow the story to be told differently and to see whether we ourselves might be in the wrong place
within it.

How might we be putting too much emphasis on our "holy" build-
ings and institutions while neglecting what God is doing outside our
"manmade" structures?

11. *Read Acts 7:54–8:3.* How is Stephen's death reminiscent of the death
of Jesus?

12. What was Saul's part in the killing of Stephen and its aftermath?

When Stephen says, "I can see heaven opened" (7:56) that doesn't
mean he could see, far up in the sky, a small door through which a
distant place might just be visible. It was more like what happens
when you've been standing on a mountain in thick cloud and suddenly a great wind sweeps away the cloud and you can see not only
the crags and peaks all around, but far away in the valley the streams

and trees and villages below. All these things had been there all the time, but you can only see them when the mist lifts. Now Stephen sees the heavenly court suddenly superimposed on the earthly one. The human judges were condemning Stephen to death, but the heavenly court was finding in his favor. This, again, from Luke's point of view, is itself part of the meaning of the whole scene. The temple was supposed to be the place where heaven and earth met. Stephen is demonstrating that heaven and earth in fact come together in Jesus and his followers.

13. How do you respond to what Stephen saw as he faced death?

PRAY

Pray that, like Moses, you will yield to the call of God at the least expected times and places. Pray that, like Stephen, you will be able to see Christ in the midst of accusations and danger, and that you will be able to forgive people who wrong you.

NOTE ON ACTS 7:42-43

In verse 42 Stephen says that God gave the Israelites over to worship the "host of heaven." What is he referring to? The prophets laid a charge against Israel that even during the wilderness years of the exodus (when according to the early books of the Bible God was providing the sacrificial system by which they might worship him), the people were in fact continuing to worship pagan gods—the host of heaven. These were presumably astral deities of various kinds as well as "Molech" and "Rephan." This quotation from Amos 5:25-27 is a damning indictment of a period that many Jews must have seen as in some ways the honeymoon period between God and Israel. It was in fact, says Amos (and Stephen), a time of rank rebellion, of idolatry rather than true worship.

8

A MAGICIAN AND
A FINANCE MINISTER

Acts 8:4-40

Philip, one of the seven deacons appointed in Acts chapter 6, seems to have quickly outgrown his purely administrative role. He has had to leave Jerusalem in a hurry following the death of Stephen, but he is by no means in hiding. This chapter of Acts concerns the remarkable doings of Philip, the deacon-turned-evangelist; and from another point of view it continues the theme of the opening up of the gospel to the non-Jewish world. Jesus was the one through whom the slow and winding story of God's people had reached its destination, and with it the moment of redemption for the whole world.

OPEN

What different circles or networks of people are you part of, and how did you become connected to them?

STUDY

1. *Read Acts 8:4-25.* Samaria, the hilly part of the country between Judea and Galilee, was home to people whom the Jews on either side

regarded with deep suspicion and hostility. The Samaritans kept to a form of Judaism but with significant elements changed. Given this background, what is remarkable about Philip's preaching and the response (vv. 5-8)?

2. Why is Simon especially captivated by certain aspects of Philip's activity (vv. 7-13)? *he was baptized but did not have the holy spirit*

3. What is the purpose of the apostles' visit from Jerusalem (vv. 14-17)? *Help receive the holy spirit*

4. When the new converts receive the Holy Spirit through the laying on of the apostles' hands, Simon becomes even more intensely interested (vv. 18-19). What is he really after?

5. Why do you think Peter gives Simon such a strong reply (vv. 20-23)? *Because he wanted to use money for God's holy spirit*

6. Consider times that you have desired the Holy Spirit's power without submitting yourself to the Spirit. What is dangerous about such an arrangement? *Your will not God's*

We are not told what happened to Simon, only that he received a dire warning and begged Peter to pray that he would be spared. Luke is not interested in Simon's fate so much as in the general point that any attempt to bring the Spirit under human control—or to think one can sell this power for money—is nonsense and is to be rejected outright.

7. *Read Acts 8:26-40.* The first non-Jew to come to faith and baptism in Luke's great story is a black man from Africa. The Ethiopian eunuch was chief finance minister to the queen Candace. It is virtually impossible that he was Jewish or a proselyte to Judaism. He was an outsider to the Jewish system, but there was something about the Jewish God and the Jewish way of life that attracted him.

   What is puzzling the Ethiopian as he travels (vv. 30-34)?

8. How does the passage from Isaiah 53 (quoted briefly in Acts 8:32-33) provide a particularly good opportunity for Philip to tell "the good news about Jesus"?

9. What is the outcome of the conversation in the chariot (vv. 36-40)?

10. As you think about this story of Philip and the Ethiopian, page through the first eight chapters of Acts. Where have we seen this theme of the gospel being opened up to ever widening circles, now including the non-Jewish world?

11. What additional circles or networks of people that you aren't already a part of (interest groups, ethnic groups, social groups, geographic groups, etc.) could you or your Christian community touch with the good news?

The prophet Isaiah had meditated deeply on the fate of Israel in exile and on the promises and purposes of God, which remained constant despite Israel's failure to be the light to the nations or even to walk in the light itself. A picture took shape: a Servant who would complete Israel's task, who would come to where Israel was and do for Israel and for the whole world what neither could do for themselves. Now Philip announced that Jesus was that Servant. No wonder the Ethiopian wanted to share in the death and resurrection of this Jesus by being baptized. When you tell the story of Israel like that, with Jesus at its climax, it opens up to include everybody, including people like him, doubly excluded and now wonderfully welcomed.

12. What do people today find puzzling in the Scriptures? Think of particular people you know and the questions you have heard them ask.

13. When invited, Philip climbed into the Ethiopian's chariot and rode along with him (v. 31). The ride gave the Ethiopian the opportunity to ask questions and gave Philip the opportunity to provide answers. How can you figuratively get into someone's chariot and ride along so that you have opportunity to tell the good news about Jesus Christ?

PRAY

Pray that you and your Christian community will follow the Holy Spirit's promptings to include ever widening circles of people. Pray that you will see—and seize—opportunities to converse with people who have questions about the Bible, and that you will use their questions to tell the good news.

9

SAUL ENCOUNTERS JESUS

Acts 9:1-31

If the death and resurrection of Jesus is the hinge on which the great door of history swung open at last, the conversion of Saul of Tarsus was the moment when all the ancient promises of God gathered themselves up, rolled themselves into a ball and came hurtling through that open door and out into the wide world beyond. The story was so important to Luke that he tells it no fewer than three times—here in Acts 9 and then again from Paul's own lips in chapters 22 and 26. Everything that Saul said and did from that moment on, and particularly everything that he wrote, flowed from that sudden, shocking seeing of Jesus.

OPEN

As you look back on your spiritual life, what one or two events seem the most significant? Why do they stand out?

STUDY

1. Saul of Tarsus had been an active and approving witness to the stoning of Stephen (Acts 7:58; 8:1). He was a highly intelligent, superbly

educated, supremely biblically literate young man. *Read Acts 9:1-9.* Put yourself in the place of Saul on his way to Damascus (vv. 1-2). What is your intention, and what emotions are stirring around inside you?

2. Still putting yourself in the place of Saul, what shocking things do you see and hear (vv. 3-6)?

3. Saul had been persecuting Christian believers. How do you explain why Jesus twice says "persecuting *me*" (vv. 4-5)?

4. Verses 8-9 reveal Saul's physical state as he went to Damascus and over the next three days. If you were Saul, what would be going through your mind during this time?

During Saul's time, Jews would meditate on the different phases of the great vision of Ezekiel 1 in which the prophet sees four-faced angels carrying something like a great chariot with wheels and flashing lights, and then a great dome or expanse above. Finally, careful not to actually say he saw God, the prophet describes a voice and a figure like a man, which had the appearance of the likeness of the glory of God.

We don't know for sure, but several scholars have suggested that Saul might have been engaging in this meditation on the way to Damascus, preparing himself to act with violence against the Christians for the glory of God. Keeping his heart focused on the divine throne-chariot, seeing the angels, then the wheels, the lights, until possibly, hopefully, he might see the glory, the face—*and the face was the face of Jesus!*

The shock, the terror, the horror, the glory, the shame all dramatically intermixed would have completely upturned Saul's expectations, undoing his world in a single stroke.

5. When has God overturned your expectations in a surprising, even shocking, way?

6. *Read Acts 9:10-31.* What is daunting about the assignment which the Lord gives Ananias?

7. Think of a daunting assignment you received from the Lord. What objections did you raise?

We don't know how Ananias became a follower of Jesus. After this Scripture passage we never hear of him again. What we do know is that he was a believer, that he knew how to listen for the voice of Jesus, that he was prepared to obey it even though it seemed ridiculously dangerous, that he went where he was sent and did what he was told. And he did it with love and grace and wisdom. You can't ask for more.

8. What is Ananias told will be Paul's mission and the consequences of that mission (vv. 15-16)?

The Lord is calling Saul for a particular task. The person to do this task, to spearhead the work of getting the message out to those outside the law, must be the one who most clearly, of all others of his generation, had been the most keen to stamp the message out. When you want to reach the pagan world, the person to do it will be a hardline, fanatical, ultra-nationalist, super-orthodox Pharisaic Jew. And some say that God doesn't have a sense of humor!

9. Trace Saul's activity and movements after his conversion. Why does he keep on the move?

10. How does Barnabas intervene on Saul's behalf (vv. 26-27)?

11. Why do the disciples send Paul to Tarsus (v. 30)?

12. Of the unbelievers you know, who seems the least likely to become a follower of Christ?

13. How will you pray for that person?

PRAY

Pray for those who, like Saul, would not be considered likely candidates to become followers of Christ, let alone leaders in announcing the message. Pray also that you will serve as an Ananias, obeying the Lord in the face of danger, and as a Barnabas, speaking up for someone whom others suspect.

NOTE ON ACTS 9:20-22

When Saul first spoke publicly after his conversion, we have (in v. 20) the first time in Acts that Jesus is referred to as the Son of God. Two verses later Paul insists that Jesus really is the Messiah (which is translated in Greek as the "Christ"). What is the relationship between these two titles? The phrase "Son of God" is not used very much in the Old Testament, but when it is it has two meanings—the people of Israel (e.g., Exodus 4:22-23) and the son of David, the Messiah himself (e.g., 2 Samuel 7:12-14). All this is rammed home in Psalm 2, which the church already adopted as speaking of Jesus (Acts 4:25-26) who would be the King of the nations of the world, not just of Israel. The same theme is echoed in Psalm 72 and 89:26-27. In and through all this and more the messianic meaning of "Son of God" was steadily being fused with the Israel meaning: the king represents his people, so that he can and must stand in for them. Very early in the Christian movement, this "Son of God" figure began to take on the character of divinity, a sense that was not clear in the Old Testament. They began to see the Messiah as God's own second self, God in human form, wisdom incarnate.

10

GOD SHOWS
NO FAVORITISM

Acts 9:32–10:48

Having inserted Saul with appropriate and violent suddenness into the narrative of the Jerusalem apostles, Luke brings us back into Peter's story. Having found his way down to Joppa, Peter will be called from there on another and more widely significant errand. But there is no such thing as a small errand in the kingdom of God. We will find that Peter was where he was on proper business from the Lord, the gospel business of healing and encouraging and building up God's people.

OPEN

When has a seemingly small errand or job for the Lord turned out to be more significant than you thought?

STUDY

1. *Read Acts 9:32-42.* What are the effects of the healing of Aeneas?

2. Who do you know who reminds you of Tabitha (Dorcas)?

3. How can we give more recognition and honor to the Tabithas of the world who are often overlooked or considered insignificant?

We have to assume that there were many others like Tabitha who lived their lives in faith and hope, bearing the sorrows of life as well as celebrating its joys, and finding in the small acts of service to others a fulfillment of the gospel within their own sphere, using traditional skills to the glory of God. Luke is right to draw our eyes to the small-scale and immediate, in case we should ever forget that these are the people who form the heart of the church. I am privileged to know plenty of Tabithas. The day before I wrote this I met one whose specialty is chocolate truffles. When I meet such people I greet them as what they are, the beating heart of the people of God.

4. *Read Acts 10:1-33.* The Roman Empire was built on relentless military power. Cornelius was a centurion, a middle-ranking Roman military officer with a hundred men under him. He was posted to Caesarea, a key port in a key strategic zone. How does this first Roman we meet in the book of Acts depart from the stereotype of a Roman officer (10:1-8)?

5. What is the message of Cornelius's vision?

6. Besides pork, there was a whole range of meat which Jews were for-

bidden to eat (see Leviticus 11). These food laws served to mark out the Jewish people from their non-Jewish neighbors, a rule reinforced by the prohibition on Jews eating with non-Jews. All of this we must keep in mind as we join Peter on the roof and watch this great sail descending from heaven with unclean food in it.

If you were Peter, what kind of emotions would you be experiencing during the vision (10:9-16)?

7. God could have communicated the gospel to Cornelius directly. Why do you think he had Peter and several other believers travel from Joppa to Caesarea to meet with Cornelius and a houseful of other people face to face?

8. What had Peter learned from his vision which prepares him to meet Cornelius?

9. Some believe this story suggests that "all religions lead to God" or even that all religions are basically the same. What evidence is there in this episode that neither Cornelius nor Peter would agree with such a viewpoint?

10. The Mosaic law contains the basic prohibitions against mixing with Gentiles. The New Testament writers, including Paul, are quite clear that the law was God's word to Israel and should be respected as such. But Paul and the others are equally clear that, in the light of

Jesus Christ, the law was to be seen as God's word *for a particular period and for a particular purpose.* This is the kind of shift in thinking which was going on as Peter went to Cornelius's house. In Jesus the Messiah of Israel, God has broken down the barrier between Jews and Gentiles, humiliating both categories (Jews, because they apparently lost their privileged position; Gentiles, because they have to acknowledge the Jewish Messiah) in order to reveal God's mercy to both.

In what ways might you or your community need to experience humility for the sake of the gospel—forgoing certain privileges or giving greater honor to others?

11. *Read Acts 10:34-48.* Now that Peter has an opportunity to tell Cornelius and the others whatever he wants, what does he highlight?

12. Peter frames his message about Jesus and the story of Israel with two wider declarations—Jesus is Lord of all (10:36) and everyone who believes in him receives forgiveness of sins through his name (10:43). How have you seen the power of these messages at work?

13. The Holy Spirit had fallen on believers in Jerusalem (Acts 2) and in Samaria (Acts 8). Now it has fallen on Gentiles in Caesarea. What is Luke emphasizing with this sequence of episodes?

PRAY

Ask God to open your eyes and your heart where you have been closed to outsiders. Pray that you will see people as God sees them, as beloved by God and in need of the gospel. Thank God for the people who first brought the message to those of your ethnic background, whether it was many centuries ago or recently.

NOTE ON ACTS 10:2

Cornelius fell in the category of a God-fearer, a Gentile who attended the synagogue and worshiped the God of Israel but who had not yet become a proselyte through circumcision and hence was not yet a full member of the community. He was described by Luke as devout, a man of regular prayer. He was a seeker after God and was generous with his money. Those he sent to Joppa told Peter that Cornelius had the respect not only of his peers in the Roman army but of the Jewish community in the neighborhood as well (10:22).

NOTE ON ACTS 10:44-45

Cornelius and his household don't even have a chance to say, "We believe." The Spirit comes upon them and they speak with tongues just as the apostles did on the day of Pentecost. There are many signs of new life recorded in Acts, of which "tongues" is only one, and it is by no means always present; but sometimes, when it happens, it happens for a purpose. Here the purpose is clear: Peter and those with him (circumcised, that is, Jewish, men) need to know that these *un*circumcised people have been regarded by the Holy Spirit as fit vessels to be filled with his presence and voice. And if that is so, there can be no barriers to baptism. All this is what is meant by the opening line of Peter's speech, "God has no favorites."

11

CONTROVERSY
AND VINDICATION

Acts 11

With what took place in the home of Cornelius, Gentiles were admitted as full members of the new and rapidly developing Jesus family without having to become Jews in the process. In his otherwise fast-paced narrative, Luke gives the story several repetitions. We can only conclude that for Luke the admission of Gentiles into God's people, without needing to take on the marks of Jewish identity (that is, circumcision and food taboos), was one of the central and most important things he wanted to convey. But just as there were anxieties and divisions already within the Jerusalem community at the start of Acts 6, so now a further and potentially more divisive split is starting to open up, which will turn within a few years into a major problem.

OPEN

How do you determine whether a new idea or movement among Christians is from the Lord or not?

STUDY

1. *Read Acts 11:1-18.* What controversy awaits Peter when he travels from Joppa to Jerusalem?

2. How does Peter respond to the objections?

3. When have you been criticized for something you did in ministry, and how did you respond?

4. Why do you think Peter's critics came to agree with him?

For the first time we encounter a group in Jerusalem who will become more and more significant as the story goes on, and who crop up for good measure in the writings of Paul: a group of Jewish believers who were insisting on the importance of circumcision. This is clearly a hard-line group *within* the Jerusalem believers, not a group of unbelieving Jewish rigorists. The phrase in verse 2 literally means "those who are of the circumcision," which could simply mean "all Jewish men." But verse 2 seems clearly to be talking about a smaller pressure group within the larger, but still Jewish, group of believers. Things were not static in the political world of Jerusalem through the forties and fifties of the first century. The law was the equivalent of the national flag at a time when the whole nation felt under intense and increasing pressure. To welcome Gentiles as equal brothers and sisters must have looked like fraternizing with the enemy.

5. *Read Acts 11:19-30.* Antioch in Syria was one of the places in the ancient world which functioned as crossroads of culture and trade. It was a great, thriving, crowded, cosmopolitan city. From this passage, what significant events happened in Antioch to make it important in the history of the early church?

6. How do you think today's meaning of *Christian* compares with what people in Antioch meant by *Christian* (v. 26)?

7. Barnabas had spoken up for Saul in Jerusalem (Acts 9:27). How does he again show his confidence in Saul (vv. 25-26, 30)?

8. What are practical ways we can encourage fellow Christians?

When Barnabas arrived in Antioch he saw the grace of God and was glad (v. 23). What he saw was not just a large and motley crowd of unlikely looking people crowding into someone's house, praising God and being taught about Jesus and the Scriptures. What he saw was God's grace at work. It took humility and faith to see that, and Barnabas had both, thanks to the work of the Holy Spirit in him.

9. Where do you see the grace of God at work? Think especially of settings which are looked down on by others.

10. Barnabas spotted Saul as the person who could teach the new believers in Antioch. The church needs not only the people who can take the work forward but the people who, in prayer and humility, can spot the very person that God is calling.

    What should we be looking for in people as we think of different types of ministry they might help in?

11. How did the Christians in Antioch show an early concern for the poor?

12. What is an immediate need for which you and your fellowship group can "send what you can" as the disciples did (vv. 29-30)?

PRAY

If you bear the name of *Christian*, pray that you will literally be a *Christ person*, one of the Messiah people, that your life will always reflect the life of Christ. Pray that you will respond to any criticism with grace and a clear and calm explanation. Thank God for people who have encouraged you in ministry and have even influenced you into particular roles.

12

THE TRUE KING RULES

Acts 12

After initial opposition from the chief priests and then persecution initiated by a zealous young Pharisee, the followers of Jesus now at last come in for royal attention. Herod Agrippa I was thought of by the Jewish population as "their man," trusted more or less by the Romans but also popular with his people. It was also strongly in Herod's interests both to show his Roman overlords that he would not tolerate dangerous movements developing under his nose and to show his own people that he was standing up, as they would have seen it, for their ancestral traditions. Herod either saw, or wanted people to think he saw, the Christian movement as a political threat. He took action at Passover time, which was thought of as the time when God delivered his people from slavery.

OPEN

What threats face Christians today, locally and around the world?

STUDY

1. *Read Acts 12:1-25.* How does Herod strike at the church (vv. 1-5)?

2. What is the church's immediate response?

3. In 12:15 the gathered believers don't believe Rhoda but think that Peter must be already dead and addressing them from beyond the grave. (While guardian angels were not an uncommon idea at the time, there is no evidence that people in those days thought they could imitate voices.)

   Why do the gathered believers have trouble believing that their prayers have been answered?

4. When have you prayed fervently and then had trouble believing that God was answering or had answered?

5. Why is it sometimes hard for us to believe that God has answered our prayers?

Luke allows us to see the early church for a moment not as a bunch of great heroes and heroines of the faith, but as the same kind of muddled, half-believing, faith-one-minute-and-doubt-the-next sort of people as most Christians we all know. Skeptical thinkers dismiss the story of Peter's release from prison as a pious legend, but nobody constructing a pious legend out of thin air would make up this ridiculous story about Rhoda (so excited she forgets to open the door) and the praying-but-hopeless church (who thinks Rhoda is mad when she says their prayers are answered). It has the ring of truth: ordinary truth, down-to-earth truth, at the very moment that it is telling us something truly extraordinary and heaven-on-earthly.

6. From this whole chapter, what can we tell about the character of Herod?

7. In this chapter what conflicts and contrasts does Luke draw explicitly and implicitly between King Herod and the true King of Israel?

8. Look over the first twelve chapters of Acts. How has Luke shown the persecution of the early believers building and finally reaching a peak in this chapter?

Things appear to go badly for the church, this way or that. There may be real reverses, tragedies and disasters. And yet the God who has revealed himself in and through Jesus remains sovereign, and his purpose is going forward whatever the authorities from without or various controversies from within may do to try to stop it. The chief priests in Jerusalem have been left spluttering angrily into their beards; Saul of Tarsus, the most prominent and violent of the Pharisaic persecutors, has been converted; and now Herod Agrippa, having had an unsuccessful attempt at killing off the church's main leadership, is himself suddenly cut down with a swift and fatal disease.

9. What difficult situations are you facing—whether physical, emotional, spiritual, financial, professional or in any other way—for which you need to offer prayer and expect God's answers?

10. How have you seen God at work even in these situations?

11. Look back over the first half of the book of Acts. What words, phrases or events strike you as you consider the story of the early church so far, and why?

12. How do those words or phrases apply to your own church fellowship?

PRAY

Pray about the situations you named for question 9. Resolve to look for and expect the Lord's answers. As you consider the first half of the book of Acts, ask the Lord to show you specific ways in which Luke's account can inspire you and your church in your own witness and service for Jesus the Messiah.

NOTE ON ACTS 12

The Herod in this chapter was a grandson of Herod the Great and half-brother of Herod Antipas, the brooding and malevolent figure of the Gospels during Jesus' years of public ministry. The full name of the king in Acts 12 is Herod Julius Agrippa, and he is sometimes referred to as Agrippa I in distinction to his son, Herod Agrippa II, whom we shall meet in Acts 25–26. Herod Agrippa I died in A.D. 44 as we know from various sources.

The Herods had no royal blood, and were not even fully Jewish, though they gave token approval to the Jewish faith. They were primarily opportunistic military commanders and politicians whom the Romans made into kings to further their own Middle Eastern agendas. The Romans had installed Herod the Great and then his sons after him as puppet monarchs to do their dirty work for them. Most Jews resented both parts of this arrangement and longed for a chance to revolt.

13

TO JEWS FIRST
AND GENTILES ALSO

Acts 13

Luke now comes to a turning point in his story. Here we are at the start of an extraordinary triple journey which will take Paul across Turkey and Greece and back again, then again once more, and finally off to Rome itself. We would much prefer the story to be one of gentle persuasion rather than confrontation. We would like it better if Paul had gone about telling people the simple message of Jesus and finding that people were happy to accept it and live by it. But there is no advance for the gospel without opposition. Christian mission is about radical transformation of life, something which was already happening all over the place in the early chapters of Acts.

OPEN

When have you known a trusted coworker or quality leader to move on to new work? What was it like for you and others?

STUDY

1. *Read Acts 13:1-12.* How would you characterize the church at Antioch (vv. 1-3)?

2. Like many Jews going out into the Greek world, Saul began to use a Greek name, *Paul*, whether because it was another name he had had all along or because it was close to his own real name. When Paul and his companions met the magician on Cyprus, what are some various ways they could have responded?

3. How does Paul respond, and with what results?

4. We live in a curious split-level world of modern skepticism on the one hand and rampant spiritual beliefs of many varieties on the other. What various spiritual beliefs are common?

   Highes Power

5. We are not all facing the kinds of situations that Paul and Barnabas faced. But what are appropriate Christian responses to the variety of supernatural beliefs and practices we might encounter today?

6. *Read Acts 13:13-43.* Paul and Barnabas, having left Antioch in Syria, now arrive in a different Antioch, this one in Pisidia in what is now south central Turkey (v. 14). It was customary in synagogue, follow-

ing the reading of the law and the prophets, to allow visitors to give a fresh word of exhortation. The instant fellowship of Jewish people around the world and the ready acceptance of previously unknown visitors to public worship provided a natural context for Paul to announce the good news.

How does Paul stress with these Jews the continuity of the story of Israel with the coming of Jesus (vv. 16-25)?

7. In the condensed amount of time which this opportunity gives him, what does Paul choose to emphasize and why?

Paul quotes Psalm 16 just as Peter did in Acts 2:27. That David's body decayed after death but Jesus' did not because of the resurrection is a sure sign that Jesus is indeed the one promised to David, and through whom God would bring the fulfillment of his promises to Israel and thus to the world.

8. How do the promises Paul mentions in 13:38-39 apply to Israel in particular as well as to other ethnic and cultural groups?

9. What do Paul and Barnabas mean when they urge their listeners to remain in God's grace (v. 43)?

10. Read Acts 13:44-52. How has Paul and Barnabas's reception changed from the previous Sabbath?

11. Why are some of the Jewish leaders filled with righteous indigna-
    tion, and why are the Gentiles thrilled?

Paul believes, of course, that what God has done in Jesus he has
done for the whole world; but he makes it very clear throughout this
address that the first stage is always to see Jesus in relation to Israel
itself. Within the hope of Israel there always lay the promise that
when God did for Israel what Israel longed for him to do, then the
Gentiles would come into the picture.

12. Why might your church or Christian community resist including
    other groups that haven't been part of your fellowship before?

13. What can be done to increase a spirit of openness?

PRAY

Pray that you and your Christian community will find ways to respond
creatively to the cafeteria of spiritual options available to people these
days. Bring to God the question of how you can encourage others to
welcome new groups of people into your fellowship.

14

Open Doors and Opposition

Acts 14

Those of us in "mainstream" denominations are, by and large, respectable. There are two things you won't find much of in our ordinary day-by-day life. You won't find much in the way of persecution. And you won't find much in the way of signs and wonders. The lows have gone, but so have the highs. As long as our churches are places where we struggle to sustain an hour or two of public worship per week, with "real life" only minimally affected by it, we will be like a bunch of vaguely religious cows in a field, mooing on Sunday mornings and chewing the cud the rest of the time. But if we really worked at trying to be for our world what the apostles were for their Jewish world, things might change!

OPEN

What is the most radical change in a person you have seen because of the gospel?

STUDY

1. *Read Acts 14:1-7.* In Iconium there is once again a mixed response to Paul's preaching, similar to what occurred in the synagogue at Antioch of Pisidia that we saw in Acts 13. In view of such strong opposition, why do you think Paul and Barnabas remained in Iconium a long time (v. 3)?

2. How does the Lord confirm the word which the disciples spoke (v. 3)?

3. The synagogue wasn't just a place of worship. It was the main community center for Jews in each locality, the place where they came together to address and settle all kinds of issues. What are the equivalent public venues today for this sort of discussion?

4. How could your fellowship engage the gospel in one or two of these venues?

5. After Paul and Barnabas get wind of a plot against them, they decide to leave Iconium (vv. 4-6). In your own experience, how do you know when to hold your ground, and when the battle is not worth pursuing?

We should be able to tell the story of our world, the story that people know is *their* story, the one they always knew they wanted to hear, so that it ends with Jesus—not artificially or like a conjurer pulling a rabbit out of a hat, but so that he appears as what and who he is: the truly human one, the one in whom are hidden all the treasures of wisdom and knowledge, the living bread through whom all our hungers are satisfied.

6. *Read Acts 14:8-20.* How do the people of Lystra misunderstand the miracle which they witness (vv. 11-13)?

7. When have you seen the Christian message misinterpreted in a startling (and perhaps even humorous) way?

8. What Paul said in the synagogue at Antioch in Acts 13 is totally unlike what he has to say now in Lystra. Why and how does it differ?

9. In what situations is it valid to present the good news differently in different situations to different people?

10. First the crowd hailed Barnabas and Paul as gods. Then suddenly they want to kill them. Why do you think the crowds turn against the apostles so abruptly (vv. 19-20)?

11. *Read Acts 14:21-28.* Paul and Barnabas go back through several cities where they had faced severe opposition. What is their purpose in returning?

12. When Paul and Barnabas laid hands on the newly appointed elders, that didn't mean they were automatically "safe." New times of testing would probably burst in on them. But the church belongs to Jesus, ministers belong to Jesus, and he is responsible for them. Everything about following Jesus, from top to bottom, is built on the belief that Jesus is Lord over the church as well as the world, and by his Spirit he calls, he equips, he guides, he warns, he rebukes, he encourages. It's his business.

Sometimes we think of Christian work as "my ministry," "our ministry," "his ministry" or "her ministry." What practical differences does it make to think of it as the Lord's ministry?

13. There is a sense of completion about verses 24-28. At least for now, Paul and Barnabas have accomplished their task and can enjoy something of a respite. When have you had a similar feeling after an intense period of giving yourself to others?

PRAY

Thank God for open doors of the Lord's ministry. Entrust yourselves and others to the Lord in whom you have believed (Acts 14:23).

NOTE ON ACTS 14:21-28

Another theme becomes evident in 14:26—the grace of God. We've seen it before in Acts 11:23 when Barnabas went to Antioch and then in 13:43 when Paul and Barnabas exhorted the believers to continue in God's grace. This is important for several reasons, one of which is that Paul's letter to the Galatians was likely written around this moment in the story Luke is telling, in other words, before the great Council of Acts 15. I'm inclined to think that the "Galatians" addressed were precisely the churches of Pisidian Antioch, Iconium, Lystra and Derbe, and that the "agitators" who had come in to disturb them by insisting on circumcision had done so fairly soon after Paul had left them behind (see Galatians 2:11). If that is so, and even if it is otherwise, then we have to say that Luke's quiet emphasis on grace corresponds closely to Paul's insistence on grace in Galatians. The new life in the gospel had nothing to do with human qualifications. It was dependent utterly on God's free gift.

DEALING WITH DISPUTES

Acts 15

Acts 15 is about controversy in the early church. We can understand Paul and Peter, who insist that God has granted Gentiles repentance that leads to life without the Gentiles needing to be circumcised (as we saw in Acts 11). And we can understand the circumcision faction, who are named more precisely as believing Pharisees in Acts 15:5; Paul was himself a believer who had belonged to the Pharisaic party. But we must be clear that Acts 15 is not simply a matter of tradition versus innovation. It is about a very specific and concrete point which is central to the whole of early Christianity: because God has fulfilled his covenant with Israel in sending Jesus as Messiah, the covenant family is now thrown open to all, without distinction.

OPEN

When have you seen a dispute among Christians settled in a Christlike way?

STUDY

1. *Read Acts 15:1-11.* What is at stake in the controversy?

2. What approach do the believers in Antioch decide to take to solve the issue?

3. How does Peter present the case for his viewpoint (vv. 6-11)?

4. *Read Acts 15:12-35.* How does the firsthand evidence of Paul and Barnabas (vv. 4, 12) affect the discussion and conclusions?

James was apparently one of Jesus' brothers, who had not believed in him during Jesus' public career (John 7:5). Jesus had appeared to James in a special and separate occasion after his resurrection (1 Corinthians 15:7) and James had joined with the apostles in prayer (Acts 1:14). By all accounts James became a prominent leader in the first generation of Christianity (Galatians 1:19 and 2:9). His judgment, summing up the debate and its results, is extremely important.

5. In verses 16-18 James quotes from Amos 9:11-12. What bearing does this Scripture have on the controversy?

6. James and the others work out in Acts 15:6-21 the double principle of *no needful circumcision* on the one hand and *no needless offense* on the other. The Gentiles who have believed in Jesus do not have to be circumcised; that is, they do not have to become Jewish in order to become Christians. They are not in a separate category when it comes to salvation. But the Gentile Christians are to be encouraged not to offer needless slaps in the face to their as-yet-unbelieving

Jewish neighbors. They should keep well away from various rituals involved in pagan worship, including the drinking of blood, ritual prostitution and other orgiastic elements that were assumed to be practiced in at least some temples some of the time. If anyone thinks that this is some kind of compromise, it is not only a compromise which stands here in Scripture itself, but it is one for which James himself argued on the basis of Scripture.

Why are Christians so often reluctant to accept a both/and compromise and instead often insist on an absolute either-or result when there is a dispute?

7. The church in Antioch needed to know beyond all doubt that Paul had not simply written this letter himself and passed it off as an official document. What steps does the Jerusalem church take to confirm the authenticity of the letter?

8. Why would the letter have delighted those who receive it (v. 31)?

9. How does the group that goes to Antioch follow up on the instructions in the letter (vv. 32-35)?

10. *Read Acts 15:36-41.* A new controversy arises in Antioch. How is it different from the circumcision controversy?

11. With one important dispute resolved, Luke ironically follows with a more personal difference of opinion that is not settled. Nonetheless, what good seems to come out of Paul and Barnabas splitting up (vv. 39-41)?

As usual in this kind of thing, both Paul and Barnabas were, in a sense, in the right. Paul was thinking back to all the opposition they had faced in Turkey. John Mark had not even made it to Turkey but had gone back home from Cyprus (Acts 13:13). Paul knew he desperately needed people he could rely on totally, whatever happened. Barnabas, the "son of encouragement" living up to his name (Acts 4:36), could no doubt see that John Mark was only a youngster and that he had simply panicked on the previous trip. Giving John Mark a second chance would show the Jerusalem church that they, Paul and Barnabas, wanted to cement the partnership between Antioch and Jerusalem which had been firmly and publicly established through the Jerusalem Council. Luke could quite easily have found a less embarrassing way of explaining the new missionary pairings.

Anyone who suggests that Luke is trying to whitewash early church history or imply that the apostles were angels should think again. By including this unhappy episode, Luke adds credibility to all he has written. I have a hunch that he told this shocking little story partly because he wanted this lesson to be heard and taken to heart. God can take the greatest human folly and sin and bring great good from it.

12. What key ideas do you see in Acts 15 that would help in dealing with disagreements among Christians?

13. How might these be applied to disagreements among believers you are facing now?

PRAY

Pray for grace and wisdom in settling arguments, whether ones where you are directly involved or ones in which you are called to play the role of mediator. Pray for anyone with whom you are in conflict.

NOTE ON ACTS 15:33-40

Those with sharp eyes will have spotted that there is no "verse 34." The earliest and best manuscripts of the New Testament have the text as we now see it. But there is a puzzle. Luke says (15:33) that Judas and Silas returned to Jerusalem; but a few verses later (15:40) Paul chooses Silas to go from Antioch on his next journey. So did Silas go back to Jerusalem or did he stay in Antioch? There is no necessary contradiction. Paul could have sent a message to Jerusalem calling Silas back. But at some point two scribes, independently, decided to tidy things up to explain what Silas did. When the New Testament verse-numbering was added centuries later, this additional material was still in the text people were using at the time and it was labeled as verse 34. All contemporary translations now omit it.

Silas is the same person as "Silvanus" who appears in the two letters Paul wrote to Thessalonica, and who is also mentioned in 2 Corinthians 1:19. Whether or not he is the same as the "Silvanus" mentioned in 1 Peter 5:12 is impossible to say.

16

INTO NEW TERRITORY

Acts 16

If you pray for wisdom about a particular decision, and then find yourself coming to a conclusion you hadn't expected, you either go with it or you decide that you didn't really mean that prayer in the first place. It is likely that Paul went through such a process before he chose Timothy as a travel companion and assistant. Paul knew he would need help of various kinds and at various stages, and after previous experiences he knew he had to have someone he could totally trust. He became convinced of that in Timothy's case.

OPEN

When did you have a decision to make and pray for wisdom? What was the result?

STUDY

1. *Read Acts 16:1-15.* Paul's missionary method, whenever he got to a new town, was to go to the Jewish synagogue first. That meant he and his companions had to be acceptable as fully fledged Jews, able to move freely among the Jewish community without putting up a

barrier. Timothy was Jewish because his mother was Jewish; but because his father was a Greek, he had not been circumcised as a baby. Paul circumcised Timothy not because Timothy needed circumcision to become a full member of God's people, but because it would be much easier to advance Paul's mission if his companions could all be seen as proper Jews. This is the opposite of what happened with Titus, a Gentile (Galatians 2:1-5).

While being very principled, apparently Paul felt that different ministry situations called for different practical approaches involving the same issue. What examples can you think of today in which this would also be true?

2. What complications arise as Paul, Silas and Timothy travel through what is now western Turkey?

3. Consider Paul's experience in verses 9-10. We don't know if this was a specific word of prophecy or a deep, growing, internal conviction. What principles can help us know whether or not we are being guided by the Lord regarding a certain decision we have to make?

4. Verse 10 is the first time "we" is used in the narrative. Why?

5. How does the Lord open the doors for the gospel in the Roman colony of Philippi?

6. Paul's habit was to begin where the local Jews were worshiping, at the synagogue. But there was no synagogue at Philippi. Somehow Paul

and his friends got wind of Jews meeting at a riverbank for prayer. It seemed to be mainly a group of women; perhaps, as with Timothy's family, it was Jewish women with Greek husbands. Not all of them were actually Jewish. Lydia was a God-fearer, a Gentile who had come to realize in Judaism something powerfully attractive and wise.

The Lord opened Lydia's heart to pay attention to the gospel (v. 14). How did the Lord open your heart in a similar way?

7. Lydia opened her home to the missionaries (v. 15). How can your home become a place of ministry?

8. Read Acts 16:16-40. The girl with a spirit that could predict the future kept shouting that Paul and Barnabas came from the most high God to announce salvation. (vv. 16-18). Now that was true; but probably not in the sense either that she meant it or that people would understand it. *God Most High* to someone living in Philippi wouldn't mean the God of Abraham, the One God of Jewish monotheism. It would mean either Zeus or whichever god they thought was at the top of the local pantheon. And *salvation* wouldn't mean what it meant to a Jew or a Christian, but "health" or "prosperity" or "rescue" from some kind of disaster (as we see in vv. 30-31).

What spiritual, social and religious attacks do the missionaries meet in Philippi (vv. 16-24)?

9. What is the scene in the prison just before and just after the earthquake (vv. 25-28)?

10. The jailer was afraid he'd be condemned for letting prisoners escape. Bishop Stephen Neill once told me that the translation that best captures the jailer's frantic question in Acts 16:30 is, "Gentlemen, will you please tell me how I can get out of this mess?" How was "believe in the Lord Jesus" the best answer to the jailer's question (and ours) of how to be rescued, at many levels?

11. What radical changes come over the jailer because of "the word of the Lord" (vv. 29-34)?

12. How does Paul's insistence on his and Silas's Roman citizenship help protect the new believers in Philippi?

13. Paul took it for granted that the resources God had given him, such as his Roman citizenship, were to be used in fulfilling his calling. This doesn't provide an easy template for all subsequent Christians to figure out how they should employ their political or civic status within their Christian vocation. That will vary from time to time and place to place. It does suggest that we should avoid easy dogmatism of this kind or that while still holding firmly to the belief that Jesus is Lord.

When and how is it appropriate for Christians to use their civic rights or status today in ministry?

PRAY

Consider new territories (whether physical or spiritual or both) where the Holy Spirit may be calling you to venture. Pray for wisdom, guidance and courage to follow the Spirit's leading. Pray that you will be equipped physically and spiritually.

17

AMONG THE PHILOSOPHERS

Acts 17

Luke has shown us how the gospel matches up against two major opponents: the zealous Jews in synagogues around Turkey and now in northern Greece, and the economic and political forces of the Roman Empire. But there is an entire world of thought which we haven't yet had on stage. This is the hugely important sphere of the prevailing ancient philosophies. They conditioned how thousands of ordinary people saw the world, what they thought of as reasonable and unreasonable, what they thought about the gods, what they thought human life was for and how best you should live it. Millions who had never studied philosophy, who maybe could not even read or write, were nevertheless deeply influenced by the major currents of thought that were debated in the schools, just as plenty of people today who have never studied philosophy or economics are massively influenced by popular media presentations of large and complex ideas.

OPEN

How would you describe the prevailing philosophy of the people around you? Or in the larger society?

STUDY

1. *Read Acts 17:1-21.* Paul follows his normal practice in going to the synagogue, where he expounded the Scriptures. But this time there is a new note. Luke says that Paul was interpreting and explaining that it was necessary for the Messiah to suffer and to rise again from the dead.

   What are the mixed results of Paul's preaching (vv. 4-6)?

2. The fact of a crucified Messiah is the major roadblock in the way of any devout Jew believing that Jesus was or could be God's anointed. How could God allow such a thing? How could God be honored thereby? And how could God do, through such a Messiah, the messianic work of bringing peace and justice to the world and rebuilding the temple? It wasn't the way many in the synagogue community wanted to understand the story of Israel.

   In what senses had Paul and Silas turned the world upside down (v. 6)?

3. How do the people in Berea differ from the people of Thessalonica?

4. Why are both openness to new ideas and a willingness to examine Scripture important together rather than emphasizing one or the other?

5. Why does the team of Paul, Silas and Timothy temporarily split up (vv. 13-15)?

6. Paul did what he usually did in the synagogue at Athens, but we have no report of the reaction. More interesting to Luke at this point, Paul argues in the marketplace, which in Athens was a marketplace of ideas as well as of other commodities. There he met the great philosophical schools of the day, the Epicureans and the Stoics. The Epicureans held that the world and the gods were a long way away from one another, with little or no communication; the result was that one should get on with life as best one could, discovering how to gain maximum pleasure from a quiet, sedate existence. The Stoics believed that divinity lay within the present world and within each human being, so that this divine force could be discovered and harnessed; virtue consisted in getting in touch with and living according to this inner divine rationality.

The invitation for Paul to speak with the Areopagus was not as friendly and innocuous as it sounds. Calling him a "babbler" or "word-scatterer" is clearly derogatory (v. 18). It wasn't a matter of, "Well, here's an interesting fellow; let's see what he has to say." It contained a doubled veiled threat. "This man," they said, "seems to be preaching of foreign divinities." This charge was most famously and classically leveled against Socrates who was tried and condemned as a result. Athens may have been interested in new ideas, but divinities from elsewhere could easily get you into serious trouble. "Are we permitted to know . . ." (v. 19) also suggests they suspect Paul of being part of a secret group and of having secret doctrines which could be a threat to their state.

What suspicions do people have or what accusations do they make regarding Christians these days?

7. *Read Acts 17:22-34.* How does Paul take what was there in the marketplace and use it to turn the people's attention to the true God revealed in Jesus Christ?

8. What differences does Paul draw between the idols and the true God?

9. As noted earlier, the Epicureans held there is simply not enough evidence for us to be able to tell whether the gods exist or not, and if they do, what if anything they want from us. What parts of Paul's address would they have substantially agreed with and what would they have found objectionable?

10. We also noted earlier that the Stoics believed that divinity lay within the present world and within each human being. What parts of Paul's address would they have agreed with and what would they have found troubling?

11. How in 17:28-29 does Paul make the case from the Greek's own poets that carved idols must be false?

12. According to Paul, how does God verify that Jesus is the coming judge (vv. 30-31)?

13. Think of someone you know who is hopeful that there is some "unknown god." How could you use the example of Paul's message at the Areopagus to help that person consider the true God revealed in Christ?

PRAY

Pray for people who are aware that there is "an unknown god" but do not know who he is or how to find him. Pray that the Holy Spirit will enlighten them with the knowledge that leads to faith. Pray that the Spirit will use you to be a channel for the knowledge of Christ.

NOTE ON ACTS 17:18

The accusation of advocating foreign gods is based on a misunderstanding Paul's listeners had of his message, which was about Jesus and the resurrection. *Resurrection*, which in Greek is *anastasis*, seems to have sounded to them like another god, or rather, since the word is feminine, a goddess: Jesus and what they supposed to be his divine female consort!

18

STAYING PUT AND TRAVELING ON

Acts 18

Luke offers us no set pattern for the way in which people come, step by step, into full membership in the Christian family and full participation in all the possibilities that are thereby open to them. Sometimes it happens this way, sometimes that. Just as humans grow to maturity at different paces, and some make great strides in one area while others have to catch up later, so it seems to be in the church. What matters is that we are open, ready to learn even from unlikely sources, and prepared for whatever God has to reveal to us through the Scriptures, the apostolic teaching and the ongoing and always unpredictable common life of the believing family.

OPEN

What different ways have people you know come to faith in Christ?

STUDY

1. *Read Acts 18:1-11.* What encouragement and what difficulties does Paul experience in Corinth?

2. When has the Lord given you confidence to stay in a situation even though it was difficult?

Whereas the last vision Paul had was of someone telling him to go somewhere he hadn't expected (Acts 16:9), in Corinth he has a vision telling him to stay put (Acts 18:9-10). Presumably Paul needed that encouragement. Visions, both in the New Testament and in much later experience, are not normally granted just for the sake of it. One of the many lessons Acts teaches quietly, as it goes along, is that you tend to get the guidance you need when you need it, not before, and not in too much detail.

3. *Read Acts 18:12-28.* What accusations are brought against Paul in Acts 18:12-13?

4. What is the reaction of the proconsul Gallio?

At least since the time of Julius Caesar, Jews had been allowed to practice their own religion and were not forced to worship the Roman gods. The question dangling over the young church at several points in Luke's narrative is this: does being a Christian mean you are acting illegally according to Roman law and custom? Or is the community of Jesus' followers rather to be seen simply as a variant of Judaism and therefore to be permitted? Gallio, who has presumably taken the trouble to inform himself both about the relevant laws and about what the new religion is up to, dismisses the charge. It is an internal matter within Judaism, not something that Roman law need bother about. Sometimes, as Luke no doubt wants us to remark once more, even pagan officials do things which genuinely and thoroughly advance the cause of the kingdom of God.

5. How does Paul's first visit to Ephesus (vv. 19-21) differ from his visit to Corinth (vv. 1-11)?

6. Luke hurries through Paul's subsequent travels (vv. 22-23) back to Antioch and then once again through Galatia (what is now south central Turkey). To prepare us for Paul's return to Ephesus, Luke introduces us to another missionary, one of those fascinating characters in early Christianity whom we wish we could get to know better: Apollos. How was Apollos uniquely equipped for ministry (vv. 24-25)?

7. Apollos knew about the baptism of John for the forgiveness of sins. What apparently did Apollos not know or understand?

8. How did Priscilla and Aquila help Apollos (v. 26)?

9. What were the results of Priscilla and Aquila's personal attention to Apollos (vv. 27-28)?

Apollos was clearly a follower of Jesus but was deficient in certain respects. The heart of what was missing for Apollos seems to be something about Christian baptism in the name of Jesus and about baptism in the Holy Spirit. Though he knows a lot about Jesus and presumably already regards him as the Messiah, he knows only John's baptism. Nobody has told him that from the Day of Pentecost onward the church had welcomed people into its full fellowship through baptism in the name of Jesus (or, as it quickly developed, in the name of the Trinity, as in Matthew 28:19).

10. Who have been your mentors or guides in the faith as Priscilla and Aquila helped Apollos, and in what ways did they help you?

11. Who are you now mentoring or who might you in turn mentor or train in the faith?

12. How can you come alongside your "Apollos," in the Christlike spirit of Priscilla and Aquila, to help that person be even more effective in ministry?

PRAY

Bring to the Lord any situations in which you are not sure whether to stay or move on. Pray that the Lord will make his will clear to you and give you the encouragement to choose the right way. Thank God for all those people who taught you the Word, and pray for continuing opportunities to teach others.

NOTE ON ACTS 18:12

Figuring out how to date Paul's life and journeys has been a notorious puzzle for many generations of scholars. Then archaeologists turned up an inscription in Delphi, a few miles northwest of Corinth. Gallio, who was the younger brother of the famous philosopher Seneca (who was himself tutor to the Emperor Nero), was proconsul of Achaea (Greece) in the second half of 51 and on into early 52, before leaving through ill health. Scholars are now more or less agreed that Paul must have appeared before him some time in late 51. The reference to Gallio has become the peg on which a good deal of the rest of Paul's chronology can hang.

NOTE ON ACTS 18:18

Luke does not explain why Paul had his hair cut. Perhaps, as is often the case in ancient history, there is an explanation which would be apparent to people at the time but which has long since ceased to be obvious to us. Perhaps Paul wanted to mark himself as clearly devout to forestall challenges from the Jews. Sometimes in Paul's world, people would make a special promise as a sign and reminder to themselves of solemn prayers and undertakings they had given to God. Perhaps, when the Lord told Paul to remain in Corinth (18:9-11), he decided to mark the moment by not having his hair cut again until he left the area. Cenchreae, where he had it cut, is the eastern port of Corinth. Since he was leaving Corinthian soil to go back to Jerusalem, now would be the appropriate time to have it cut.

19

CLASH OF POWERS AT EPHESUS

Acts 19

Paul had spent a day or two in each of the Galatian churches. He had stayed a few days in Philippi, a few weeks in Thessalonica, a day or two in Berea, a few days in Athens. Then he had spent eighteen months in Corinth. Now, as a kind of climax to his work, he is in one of the major centers of the Mediterranean world, Ephesus, a great city at the hub of the trade routes of the world, full of culture and money and temples and politics and soldiers and merchants and slaves. And power. Everything we know about Ephesus indicates that it was a place where not only social and civic power but also religious and spiritual power were concentrated. Perhaps that is why Luke begins his account of Paul's work there with a story about a fresh outpouring of the Holy Spirit. There must be nothing secondhand about the Spirit's power when you are faced with the powers of the world.

OPEN

Describe someone you've observed who was powerful—whether physically, politically, economically or spiritually.

STUDY

1. *Read Acts 19:1-22.* What is missing in the lives of the disciples Paul finds in Ephesus (vv. 1-3)?

2. In what sense might these twelve or so people have been "disciples"?

3. What difference would it make in your life if the Holy Spirit was missing?

Not only have these people in Ephesus not received the Holy Spirit; they haven't heard that there is a Holy Spirit, now freely available for all who trust in Jesus, or that Jesus was not just a follower or successor of John the Baptist but the decisive person to whom John had been pointing. They therefore need full Christian baptism and, with it, the Holy Spirit. The main thing Luke is doing in this little story is to introduce Paul's work in Ephesus and to show that, from the very beginning, he was concerned with the Spirit's powerful work both in the lives of individuals and out into the wider community.

4. How is Paul's experience in Ephesus (19:8-10) similar to his experience in Corinth (Acts 18:1-8)?

5. How do the exorcists misunderstand the power of God (vv. 13-16)?

6. What does the evil spirit's remark reveal?

7. Why do you think the humiliation of the exorcists had such a wide-reaching effect (vv. 17-20)?

Ephesus was a center of power: magic power, political power, religious power. And Paul's ministry demonstrated that the power of the name of the Lord Jesus is stronger than all of them. It is possible that the sons of Sceva were Jews who, living in pagan territory for a long time, had developed a kind of mixed economy of Jewish and pagan religion, ritual and magic. The gospel does indeed provide power, *but it is not "magic."* Magic attempts to gain that power without paying the price of humble submission to the God whose power it is.

8. *Read Acts 19:23-41.* Why do the silversmiths see Paul and his message as a threat (vv. 23-27)?

9. Does the gospel present a similar threat today? If so, how?

10. Imagine that you are caught up in the crowd in the amphitheater (vv. 29-34). What do you see, hear and think? What are your emotions?

11. How does the town clerk show wisdom (vv. 35-41)?

12. The rushing together of the economic, religious and cultural impact of the gospel is one of the major issues that Christians are having to grapple with once more in our time. Our challenge is to be so definite in our witness to the powerful name of Jesus that people will indeed find their vested interests radically challenged, while at the same time being so innocent in our actual behavior that there will be nothing to accuse us of.

What is the balance between ineffective preaching of a "gospel" which makes no impact on real life and a noisy, obstreperous, personally and socially offensive proclamation?

PRAY

Pray that the power of God will be evident in your life, not as a demonstration for its own sake or for your sake, but as a natural result of submission to God.

NOTE ON ACTS 19:24-28

Artemis is the Greek name for the Roman goddess Diana. She was the most powerful divinity in the area. In the distant past a meteorite had smashed into the surface of the earth somewhere near Ephesus, and the local people had regarded it as a gift from heaven, a statue (though presumably not very lifelike) of the goddess herself. The temple of Artemis was massive and her cult—run entirely by female officials—was the religious center of the whole area. Images of Artemis, large and small, dominated the city. Archaeologists have found dozens of them.

20

MEETINGS AND FAREWELLS

Acts 20:1–21:14

Alongside continual trial and vindication, *the journey* is the other great theme that Luke is tapping into as he tells his story, particularly his story of Paul. Few people today spend most of their lives on the move. We nevertheless feel the power and pull of a story which enables us to reflect on the journey through time which we are all making. The journey of our lives has many twists and turns. We carry memories of "where we've been" in the sense of what has happened to us. We carry hopes and fears for "where we might go next" in the sense of what may yet happen to us. Even if we live on the same street all our life long, we are on a journey whether we like it or not; and we greatly value stories that help us to see that.

OPEN

On the journey of your life, what stands out about where you've been, where you are now or where you might go next?

STUDY

1. *Read Acts 20:1-12.* Here begins another "we" passage where the author is particularly keen on telling about the group's travels in considerable detail. What are Paul's movements after he leaves Ephesus?

2. What does Luke say are Paul's purposes in his travels?

Two of Paul's most powerful letters emerge from this period. He was writing 2 Corinthians, it seems, while on the way around northern Greece (20:1-2) before ending up in Corinth. Then, while at Corinth, he wrote his masterpiece, the letter to Rome. Perhaps part of the reason for the enlarged company representing so many churches (20:4) is that Paul was collecting money from the Greek churches to give to the poor Christians in Jerusalem (which he discusses at length in 2 Corinthians 8–9 and which he mentions specifically in 24:27-18). He may have wanted the safety of a larger group of traveling companions when carrying a substantial amount of money and the clear accounting of several who could witness that the money had safely reached its destination.

3. After a passage which summarizes several months of activity over a wide area (20:1-6), why do you think Luke slows down his account to tell such a detailed story of Eutychus (20:7-12)?

4. *Read Acts 20:13-38.* What is driving Paul forward in his journey (20:13-16)?

5. Paul summons the elders of the Ephesian church to meet him at
    Miletus (20:17). As he speaks to them, Paul reflects on his time in
    Ephesus, the longest period he has ever spent with a church, and
    on his pattern of ministry and its significance. What is the mood,
    substance and purpose of what he says about the past and the future
    in verses 18-27?

6. Paul continues his address to the Ephesian elders. What dangers
    would threaten the church at Ephesus, and what would protect them
    (20:28-32)?

7. What dangers threaten your church and the church worldwide?

8. What example had Paul set for the Ephesian church (20:33-35)?

9. In what ways might we apply his example today?

According to Paul, Jesus said "It is more blessed to give than to receive" (20:35). The words do not appear in any of the four Gospels.
As John says at the end of his Gospel, there were many other things
which Jesus did, and presumably which he said, which are not written down (John 21:25). The quote sounds like the sort of thing
which might have come in the Sermon on the Mount or a similar
address. It makes sense not only as a statement by Jesus of how his

followers ought to behave but as a statement about his own manner of life. Paul followed the pattern of Jesus. Nobody would ever be able to say that Paul used his biblical learning, patient study or rhetorical gifts to feather his own nest. He had lived out the message of the gospel as he had understood it, the message of God's grace, which isn't primarily a theory but an image-bearing way of life.

10. The Ephesian elders react with tears and grief to Paul's departure, especially his words about never seeing them again. What does this communicate about the character of his ministry and the kind of person Paul was?

11. *Read Acts 21:1-14.* What urgent warnings does Paul meet as he travels?

12. As far as we can tell, what was Paul's mood as he traveled?

13. Paul's friends in Caesarea eventually accepted his decision to go to Jerusalem and said "May the Lord's will be done" (21:14), echoing Jesus' words in the Lord's Prayer and in Gethsemane. What are some situations right now for which you may need to say "May the Lord's will be done"?

PRAY

Pray that your motives and the motives of your Christian leaders for being active in ministry will be pure and never selfish. Pray for protection for the flock of your own fellowship, that no one will be drawn away by distortions (Acts 20:30).

NOTE ON ACTS 21:4

Luke is quite happy to report that the urgings of the disciples for Paul to stay were in the Spirit, without telling us how he reconciles that with the fact that Paul is clear that it is his vocation to go. Sometimes the Holy Spirit gives people enough information to know what is likely to await them but leaves them with the responsibility of deciding whether or not to go anyway.

SHOWDOWN IN JERUSALEM

Acts 21:15–22:30

It seems that everywhere Paul goes, there is a riot. That is because he is being loyal to the true, if extraordinary and dangerous, purposes of the God of Abraham, Isaac and Jacob, the creator God who will one day call the whole world to account. Riots in Antioch, stoning in Lystra, beatings in Philippi, more riots in Thessalonica, run out of town in Berea, court cases and anti-Jewish violence in Corinth, and then that escapade with thousands of chanting pagans in Ephesus. The leaders in Jerusalem, therefore, had a good idea what to expect when Paul visited them.

OPEN

When have you seen the gospel cause conflict? What was the outcome?

STUDY

1. *Read Acts 21:15-36.* After an initially enthusiastic welcome to Jerusalem, what concerns do the believers express over Paul's arrival (21:17-25)?

2. How does Paul respond to their concerns, and what do you think
   motivates him?

The church leaders in Jerusalem described the thousands of new
Jewish Christians as "zealous for the law." Apparently they were
righteously indignant for God's honor, for the eternal and unbreak-
able law of Moses, for the sanctity of the temple and the land. People
also had been spreading rumors that not only had Paul been telling
Gentile converts that they don't need to be circumcised but he had
been telling Jews to abandon their ancestral traditions and customs
as well (21:21). That latter is something Paul has neither said nor
done. And these are the *Christians* in Jerusalem! But as far as they
are concerned, it's all or nothing. Either you say that circumcision
matters, in which case every Christian has to be circumcised; or you
say it doesn't matter, in which case no Christian—including Jewish
Christians—should be circumcised.

3. How well does the church leaders' plan for Paul work? What happens in 21:27-36?

4. As much as possible, put yourself in the place of Paul in this passage.
   What are you trying to do and say?

Tribunes in the Roman army were often young men on their way up
the ladder politically and perhaps socially. But nothing in the Roman system could have prepared this tribune for the intricacies of
first-century Jewish political and religious life. The tribune would
have been in charge of the guard in the fortress Antonia, which the
Romans had built overlooking the temple compound precisely so

they could keep an eye on this kind of disturbance. It is a miracle that Paul survived. If a crowd is intent on killing someone, they can often succeed before the time it would take for an officer upstairs in the fort to notice, to call reinforcements and to hurry down to intervene. By that time they had dragged Paul out of the temple gate and "the gates were shut." That was the last time Paul would see the inside of the beautiful temple. In only another fifteen years or so, it would be destroyed, never to be rebuilt.

5. *Read Acts 21:37–22:22.* Paul has just been beaten and narrowly escaped being killed by a mob. Soldiers are carrying him into their barracks. Paul is in a vulnerable, even helpless position. How does he manage to take command of the situation (21:37-40)?

6. This is Paul's chance to do in Jerusalem what he had done in so many other places, to speak to his fellow countrymen, his beloved if misguided fellow Jews, of their own Messiah. How does Paul establish his credentials with the Jewish crowd (22:1-5)?

7. Imagine that you are one of the crowd hearing Paul tell the story in 22:6-11. How do you react and why?

People then and now have tried to find any explanation for Paul's experience other than the one which means that it actually happened, that Jesus really is alive and addresses people and transforms them from persecutors into preachers. Paul is not finished with his story, but he has staked out the ground. He has spoken the Name. Now Jesus has led him to face a mob of people just like the person he himself had been.

8. Why is the crowd willing to hear what Paul emphasizes about his time in Damascus and then Jerusalem in Acts 22:12-20?

9. What causes them to cut off Paul's defense with such a violent reaction in 22:21-22?

As Paul wrote in Romans 9–11, written only weeks before this uproar, his fellow Jews have a zeal for God, but it is not enlightened (Romans 10:1-3). They are ignorant of God's righteousness, that is, of what God is doing in the world and in their own history, and supremely in Jesus as the revelation in action of his own faithfulness to the covenant. If only they would stop and reflect, for just a moment, that God had promised that through the Messiah the Gentiles would share in *their* promises, *their* patriarchs, *their* covenants. Only a hope like that can explain the apparent folly of Paul's attempt to communicate to them the new world Jesus had inaugurated.

10. What hope do you find in Jesus that might seem like folly to others?

11. *Read Acts 22:23-30.* How does Paul show wisdom in this tight situation?

Here is a pattern we have seen regularly in Acts. When cooler heads, cooler Roman heads in particular, have a chance to prevail, Paul is vindicated of the charges leveled against him. Paul was well qualified for the work God had for him: a Jew of the strictest pedigree and highest biblical training; a Greek speaker and thinker thoroughly at home with the world of ancient philosophy and rhetoric; and a Roman citizen who knew his rights under the law and was determined to use them as necessary.

12. How has the Lord equipped you for his work?

PRAY

Give thanks to God for the hope he has given you. Ask God to guide you in how you might use the gifts he has equipped you with for the sake of his kingdom.

NOTE ON ACTS 22:25-27

Did Paul have to prove his Roman citizenship? There were severe punishments for anyone claiming untruthfully to be a citizen. Some sources say you could even be put to death for it. But in fact there was a way of proving it. It may seem unlikely that Paul still had the proof about his person after all he'd just been through, but there was an official badge, a little double-faced tablet, made of bronze most likely, known as a "diploma." It functioned both as a birth certificate and as a citizenship token. This may be another example of Luke assuming his readers would know what was going on without him being explicit. If I say, "I went through customs," I may not mention that I showed my passport even though people listening would certainly have known that I did so.

Speculation abounds about how Paul might have been a citizen since birth. Antony, the famous Roman general and politician, had granted some Jews citizenship after they had helped him in his campaigns in the middle of the first century B.C. Further back, there is evidence for a Jewish presence in Tarsus in the 170s B.C. and for some Jews there becoming Roman citizens at least a hundred years before Paul's day. So it is perfectly possible that Paul's citizenship was inherited, not just by him, but by his father and even grandfather before him.

SCHEMES AND RESCUES

Acts 23–24

For Paul, under arrest in Jerusalem, the moment of crisis becomes the moment of vision. As in Corinth (Acts 18:9-10), so now in Jerusalem, the Lord will stand by Paul. These moments of realization, of clarity of inner sight, have been all-important for Paul, just as they have been for countless Christians ever since. We Christians often sell ourselves short by quietly forgetting these moments or not talking about them for fear other people won't understand or will think we're making it all up.

OPEN

When have you felt that the Lord gave you special insight or comfort? What difference did it make?

STUDY

1. Not comprehending why the Jews find Paul so inflammatory, the Roman tribune arranges to bring him before the chief priests and the Sanhedrin, the Jewish high court (Acts 22:30). *Read Acts 23:1-35.* As he stands before them in 23:1-5, how does Paul balance re-

spect for the governing authorities with the challenges he has to offer them?

2. How in 23:6-10 does Paul get to the heart of the issue while once again showing himself to be wise as a serpent and innocent as a dove in dealing with the political powers at work?

3. When the Lord stands beside Paul the following night (23:11), it is a key turning point in Luke's story. Paul is not, after all, going to die in Jerusalem. His sense of vocation, to go to Rome, was genuine. He isn't promised a comfortable ride. But he will get there, and he must do there what he has done here: to bear witness. And the word for *witness*, as we have seen before, is the word from which we get *martyr*.

Just as Paul was receiving a word from the Lord telling him that he would make it safely to Rome, a boy happened to be at the right place at the right time, pricked up his ears and knew what to do (23:12-22). This is illustrative, perhaps, of William Temple's famous saying, "When I pray, coincidences happen; when I stop praying the coincidences stop happening."

How do you understand or how have you experienced the relationship of prayer, "coincidence" and God's work in the world?

4. In what ways is Claudius Lysias being very politically savvy in his letter to Felix (23:26-30)?

The full machinery of the Roman army, just what a traveling apostle would normally want to avoid, is mustered to rescue Paul from the plot against his life and take him to the governor, who will keep him safe. The guards who had just previously been ready to tie up Paul and flog him are now transformed into his protectors. The purpose was that Paul would make it to Rome to bear witness to Jesus (Acts 23:11).

5. *Read Acts 24:1-27.* Several specific charges are made against Paul in 24:2-8. Why would they carry so much weight with the Romans and with the Jews?

Luke has been writing the story of the early church, and particularly Paul, in terms of a succession of "trials." The gospel is all about God putting the world right—his doing so in Jesus, his doing so at the end, and his doing so for individuals in between, as both a sign and a means of what is to come. Luke wants his readers to see the life of the church itself in that same way. We shouldn't imagine that people will leave us alone, will not challenge us as to what we are doing, as to how our faith belongs in the public world. If we are the people in and through whom God is putting into effect the setting-right that happened in Jesus, and anticipating the setting-right that will happen at the end, we should expect to see that uncomfortable but necessary setting-right going on all over the place, sometimes in martyrdom and sometimes in vindication and acquittal, as the church makes its way in the world.

6. How does Paul deny some of the charges, and what does he admit to (24:10-21)?

In his defense before Felix, Paul claims the moral, theological and biblical high ground. For him, following Jesus is not an odd hobby that might lead him away from Scripture and tradition, but it is the way, indeed the Way, by which the one true God has fulfilled all that the Scriptures had said. Paul, in other words, is claiming to be a loyal and faithful Jew. For Paul, the knowledge of God in the face of Jesus the Messiah meant not that he was abandoning the faith of his ancestors but that he was penetrating to its very heart.

7. At this period the Christians did not have a standard word for themselves, and nobody else knew what to call them either. Paul uses the term *the Way* (24:14; see also Acts 9:2; 16:17; 18:25-26; 19:9, 23; 24:22). Why is *the Way* a fitting term for following Christ?

8. How would you account for Felix's inconsistent treatment of Paul (24:22-27)?

9. Why would justice, self-control and the coming judgment be such disconcerting subjects (24:25)?

10. Paul was kept in custody by Felix for two years, then was left in prison when Felix left office (24:27). Imagine yourself in Paul's position during this time. What conflicting thoughts and feelings would you be having?

11. Think of a time when you were waiting for an extended period, an in-between time. What were your thoughts and prayers then?

12. In times when it seems everything is on hold and nothing positive is happening, how can Paul's experience be of practical help for you?

PRAY

Thank God for the times you have been rescued from danger, whether physical or spiritual or both. Pray about the ways in which you feel you are still waiting for God to act. Ask God for comfort, wisdom, patience, and the assurance that he is still working and still faithful to his promises.

NOTE ON ACTS 23:24–24:27

Felix was born a slave. After being given his freedom he, with his brother Pallas, became favorites of the Emperor Claudius. This might have been because Claudius, naturally afraid as many emperors were of envious people in high places, preferred to employ and to trust people whose personal gratitude to him was so great that they would be less likely to rebel. We know his term in office in Judea ran roughly A.D. 52-59, not least because of coins which successive governors issued, with their own name and that of the emperor on them. This helps us date this whole episode with Paul. We also know that during this time things went from bad to worse. The Jews were given more and more reasons to hate their Roman overlords and to fan the flames of their zeal for God and the law. By the end of the next decade, the zeal would bring war and their utter ruin.

"I APPEAL TO CAESAR"

Acts 25–26

Sometimes when we pray and wait for God to act, part of the answer is that God is indeed going to act, but he will do so through our taking proper human responsibility in the matter. There are times when the answer is "The Lord will fight for you, and you have only to keep still" (Exodus 14:14). Other times the answer is "Be strong and very courageous, for you shall put this people in possession of the land I swore to give them" (Joshua 1:6). Discerning and discovering which applies in which case is a major element in the discernment to which all Christians, and especially all Christian leaders, are called. At this point in Paul's life, he has been promised by God through his sense of vocation (Acts 19:21) and has been promised by Jesus through a vision (Acts 23:11) that he will get to Rome. Now Paul himself has to take responsibility, at one level, for making this happen.

OPEN

In your own experience how have you discerned when to "keep still" and allow the Lord to act, and when to take the initiative and take action? Looking back, would you do any of it differently now and why?

STUDY

1. *Read Acts 25.* Paul has been in custody in Caesarea, out of the Jewish leaders' sight, for two years (Acts 24:27). What new threat to Paul do the Jewish leaders plan as soon as the new governor Festus arrives, and how is it thwarted (25:1-6)?

2. What does Paul apparently hope to accomplish by appealing to Caesar?

Paul knows his rights. Once again he protests his innocence. He insists not only on justice but on properly constituted officials doing their properly authorized job, just as he insisted on getting his public apology from the magistrates at Philippi (Acts 16:35-39). The appeal to Caesar was not like an appeal today, when a verdict has already been reached. The case against Paul has still not been tried and has still not reached a verdict, far less a sentence. What Paul is appealing for is for the case to be tried elsewhere, in the highest court in the empire.

3. We have already met Herod Agrippa I in Acts 12. This is his son Herod Agrippa II, a great-grandson of Herod the Great and popular with both the Romans and the Jews. It is fascinating to see Paul and his beliefs and preaching through the eyes of a Roman official. Festus's summary shows how the Christian faith appeared to one pagan outsider. How is Paul's case explained to Agrippa from Festus's point of view (25:13-27)?

4. How do you think nonbelievers misunderstand your Christian beliefs?

5. How can you make things more clear to them?

6. *Read Acts 26.* As Paul begins his defense in 26:1-11, what connections does he make between Christian faith and the Jewish religion?

7. For a third and final time in Acts, we hear the story of Paul on the road to Damascus. What are the distinct elements of his mission and message to the Gentiles that Jesus gives to Paul, as recounted by Paul in 26:12-18?

8. How does Paul then claim that he is fulfilling rather than undermining the most ancient traditions and richest hopes of his people (26:19-23)?

9. Agrippa cleverly avoids giving a direct answer to Paul's question in 26:27. Why would it be difficult for Agrippa to answer either yes or no?

10. What makes people reluctant today to speak either clearly for or against Jesus?

11. For the final time in Acts (here in 26:31-32), an official appointed by Rome vindicates Paul of wrongdoing against Rome. We have seen this at Philippi (16:25-40), in Corinth (18:14-17), a form of it in Ephesus (19:35-41) and in Jerusalem (23:26-31). Now Paul is heading to Caesar for his final trial, a trial which is itself not recounted in Acts. What may all this indicate about who Luke hoped would read his book?

12. What personally strikes you most about Paul in these two chapters, and why?

PRAY

Pray that you will be able to discern when to wait for the Lord to act and when to take action yourself. Pray that God will show you how Paul's example can be a guide for you in difficult situations.

THE VOYAGE TO ROME

Acts 27–28

The Jews were not (except for some fishermen) a seafaring race. They left that to the Egyptians to the south and the Phoenicians to the north, not to mention the Greeks. For the Jews, the sea was a monster. Yes, the one God had made it just as he made everything else, and it was his, and did his bidding. But all the same the sea was seen as a dark force, a power in its own right and a place from which dark powers might emerge. Paul, unusually for a Jew, was a seasoned sea traveler. He would have been under no illusions about what might await him on the long voyage to get to Rome from one of its farthest outposts. He had lived much of the last few years in that in-between stage, knowing that the sea was still potentially a great enemy while believing that all enemies had been defeated by Jesus the Messiah.

OPEN

As you have set about answering God's call and doing his will, what difficulties or obstacles have gotten in the way?

STUDY

1. *Read Acts 27.* The Fast (the day of atonement) mentioned in 27:9 was on October 5 in A.D. 59, the likely year of the journey. Sailing started to get dangerous in the eastern Mediterranean in mid-September, and normally stopped altogether by mid-November. Ships ought to be making for land, and reckoning on a long stay before the seas are safe again in spring.

   Consider Paul's behavior throughout this eventful part of the voyage toward Rome. What do his actions and words tell you about his attitudes toward the others on the ship, toward his own destiny and toward the Lord?

2. How has Luke woven in themes and images of death, rescue, being saved and breaking of bread into this episode?

3. Some Christians have been taught that once they have faith everything ought to flow smoothly. What would Acts have to tell us about that?

   The reader with an alert biblical memory may be thinking, "Where have I heard something like this before?" And the answer, which Luke certainly intends us to pick up, is the story of Jonah. Jonah was running away to Tarshish to avoid having to go and preach to the great imperial city of Nineveh. When the great storm came, the sailors did what Paul's sailors did: they threw the cargo into the sea (Jonah 1:4-5). At that point Jonah was in the hold, fast asleep, but they woke him up and ended up throwing him overboard. And of course part of Luke's point is that Paul is not Jonah; he is not running away; he is being faithful to his calling to preach in the great imperial capital to which he is bound; he is certainly not going to be thrown overboard. Instead, in a dramatic reversal, he tells the ship's company to cheer up. Paul's vision (Acts 27:23-25) is the turning point in the story.

4. How has God sustained and encouraged you in difficult times?

The idea of the church as a little ship was probably not invented at this stage, but Luke was there already. The storms do not mean that the journey is futile. They merely mean that Jesus is claiming the world as his own, and that the powers of the world will do their best to resist.

5. *Read Acts 28.* Besides saving the lives of Paul and the rest of the people on board, what opportunities does the shipwreck on Malta provide for Paul?

6. When has God given you unexpected opportunities to serve him?

7. What are some opportunities for service which you might be overlooking right now?

8. The sea and the snake have done their worst and are overcome. New creation is happening, and the powers of evil cannot stop it. Paul may arrive in Rome a more bedraggled figure than he would have liked, but the gospel which he brings is flourishing, and nobody can stop it.

   What evidence do you see that the gospel has already had an impact in and around Rome?

9. Everything Paul had done in his life was a preparation for the moment when he was to stand before Caesar. We want to know what happens when he arrives in Rome. Now what seems like an interlude in Luke's story turns out to be the major closing scene of the book. Paul invites the local Jewish leaders to come to his lodgings. Why does Paul take the initiative with the leaders of the Jews in Rome (28:17-28)?

10. As you think back over the entire book of Acts, what events and themes stand out for you?

11. The book of Acts has one of the strangest endings of any biblical book, not counting Mark whose ending is almost certainly missing. How do you react to the way the book actually ends?

12. There are many possible explanations for the book's seemingly unfinished nature. But perhaps it is deliberate. Perhaps it is an unfin-

ished story that leaves the reader facing this question: "What are you going to do about this?" How would you answer that?

The book of Acts may or may not have been written to serve a particular purpose in relation to Paul. But the real hero of the book is of course the Jesus who was enthroned as the world's Lord at the beginning and is now proclaimed, at the end, openly and unhindered, with all boldness and with nobody stopping him. Jesus of Nazareth continues to do and to teach, continues to announce the kingdom of God which has been decisively inaugurated on earth as in heaven.

PRAY

Pray that your heart will always be open to the Lord, that your ears and eyes will never be closed to him, and that he will be proclaimed openly as you live from day to day.

NOTE ON ACTS 27

Luke's Gospel begins by addressing the book to Theophilus. So does Acts. In Luke Jesus went on a journey and eventually arrived in Jerusalem. So did Paul in Acts. In the Gospel, Jesus was picked up by the Jewish authorities and handed over to the Romans. In Acts, Paul was too. Jesus was interrogated by the Roman governor, who at one point brought him before Herod Antipas. Paul was interrogated by two Roman governors and brought before Herod Agrippa. Jesus was sent to his death. Paul was sent to Rome.

In particular, Paul was sent to Rome via the sea. We must note that the ancient Jews viewed the sea as a dark force, a place from which dark powers might emerge (see, for example, Job 7:12; Psalm 69:14-15; 74:13-14; 77:16; 144:7; Daniel 7:3; Habakkuk 3:15—and the book of Jonah, of course). Acts 27 is, in other words, the equivalent of Luke 23. Paul's shipwreck corresponds to Jesus' crucifixion within Luke's narrative structure. Why does Luke do this?

This is how he conveys to us the meaning of the cross—not so much through a formula like Mark 10:45 but through the very texture of his entire narrative. In Luke there is a long buildup of warnings against Israel. Then we discover that Jesus identifies with the nation of Israel. To our horror, we watch as the judgment Jesus had prophesied for the nation, at the hands of the Romans, falls on himself.

Likewise there are clear signs and warnings building in Acts. Late fall is no time to be out on the open sea. There are strong contrary winds making travel difficult and dangerous (27:7-9). Paul himself gives a warning which was ignored (27:10-11). Then Paul breaks bread and gives thanks to God in the midst of a huge storm (Acts 27:27-35)—so reminiscent of Jesus breaking bread as a different type of storm arose around him.

Luke is not saying that Paul's experience was redemptive too or that Jesus' death was merely exemplary. Rather Luke is asking us to watch as the story unfolds, to see this narrative as it were superimposed on the story of the cross, not as just another example of suffering and vindication but as a sign of *the way the unique event of Jesus' death is implemented in the mission of the church to the world, the world as it yearns for its new creation.*

GUIDELINES FOR LEADERS

My grace is sufficient for you.
(2 Corinthians 12:9)

If leading a small group is something new for you, don't worry. These sessions are designed to flow naturally and be led easily. You may even find that the studies seem to lead themselves!

This study guide is flexible. You can use it with a variety of groups—students, professionals, coworkers, friends, neighborhood or church groups. Each study takes forty-five to sixty minutes in a group setting.

You don't need to be an expert on the Bible or a trained teacher to lead a small group. These guides are designed to facilitate a group's discussion, not a leader's presentation. Guiding group members to discover together what the Bible has to say and to listen together for God's guidance will help them remember much more than a lecture would.

There are some important facts to know about group dynamics and encouraging discussion. The suggestions listed below should equip you to effectively and enjoyably fulfill your role as leader.

PREPARING FOR THE STUDY

1. Ask God to help you understand and apply the passage in your own life. Unless this happens, you will not be prepared to lead others. Pray too for the various members of the group. Ask God to open

your hearts to the message of his Word and motivate you to action.

2. Read the introduction to the entire guide to get an overview of the topics that will be explored.

3. As you begin each study, read and reread the assigned Bible passage to familiarize yourself with it. This study guide is based on the For Everyone series on the New Testament (published by SPCK and Westminster John Knox). It will help you and the group if you have on hand a copy of the companion volume from the For Everyone series both for the translation of the passage found there and for further insight into the passage.

4. Carefully work through each question in the study. Spend time in meditation and reflection as you consider how to respond.

5. Write your thoughts and responses in the space provided in the study guide. This will help you to express your understanding of the passage clearly.

6. It may help to have a Bible dictionary handy. Use it to look up any unfamiliar words, names or places. The glossary at the end of each New Testament for Everyone commentary may likewise be helpful for keeping discussion moving.

7. Reflect seriously on how you need to apply the Scripture to your life. Remember that the group members will follow your lead in responding to the studies. They will not go any deeper than you do.

LEADING THE STUDY

1. At the beginning of your first time together, explain that these studies are meant to be discussions, not lectures. Encourage the members of the group to participate. However, do not put pressure on those who may be hesitant to speak—especially during the first few sessions.

2. Be sure that everyone in your group has a study guide. Encourage the group to prepare beforehand for each discussion by reading the

introduction to the guide and by working through the questions in each study.

3. Begin each study on time. Open with prayer, asking God to help the group to understand and apply the passage.

4. Have a group member read aloud the introduction at the beginning of the discussion.

5. Discuss the "Open" question before the Bible passage is read. The "Open" question introduces the theme of the study and helps group members to begin to open up, and can reveal where our thoughts and feelings need to be transformed by Scripture. Reading the passage first will tend to color the honest reactions people would otherwise give—because they are, of course, supposed to think the way the Bible does. Encourage as many members as possible to respond to the "Open" question, and be ready to get the discussion going with your own response.

6. Have a group member read aloud the passage to be studied as indicated in the guide.

7. The study questions are designed to be read aloud just as they are written. You may, however, prefer to express them in your own words.

   There may be times when it is appropriate to deviate from the study guide. For example, a question may have already been answered. If so, move on to the next question. Or someone may raise an important question not covered in the guide. Take time to discuss it, but try to keep the group from going off on tangents.

8. Avoid answering your own questions. An eager group quickly becomes passive and silent if members think the leader will do most of the talking. If necessary repeat or rephrase the question until it is clearly understood, or refer to the commentary woven into the guide to clarify the context or meaning.

9. Don't be afraid of silence in response to the discussion questions. People may need time to think about the question before formulating their answers.

10. Don't be content with just one answer. Ask, "What do the rest of you think?" or "Anything else?" until several people have given answers to the question.

11. Try to be affirming whenever possible. Affirm participation. Never reject an answer; if it is clearly off-base, ask, "Which verse led you to that conclusion?" or again, "What do the rest of you think?"

12. Don't expect every answer to be addressed to you, even though this will probably happen at first. As group members become more at ease, they will begin to truly interact with each other. This is one sign of healthy discussion.

13. Don't be afraid of controversy. It can be very stimulating. If you don't resolve an issue completely, don't be frustrated. Explain that the group will move on and God may enlighten all of you in later sessions.

14. Periodically summarize what the group has said about the passage. This helps to draw together the various ideas mentioned and gives continuity to the study. But don't preach.

15. Conclude your time together with the prayer suggestion at the end of the study, adapting it to your group's particular needs as appropriate. Ask for God's help in following through on the applications you've identified.

16. End on time.

Many more suggestions and helps for studying a passage or guiding discussion can be found in *How to Lead a LifeGuide Bible Study* and *The Big Book on Small Groups* (both from InterVarsity Press/USA).

Other InterVarsity Press Resources from N. T. Wright

The Challenge of Jesus
N. T. Wright offers clarity and a full accounting of the facts of the life and teachings of Jesus, revealing how the Son of God was also solidly planted in first-century Palestine. *978-0-8308-2200-3, 202 pages, hardcover*

Resurrection
This 50-minute DVD confronts the most startling claim of Christianity— that Jesus rose from the dead. Shot on location in Israel, Greece and England, N. T. Wright presents the political, historical and theological issues of Jesus' day and today regarding this claim. Wright brings clarity and insight to one of the most profound mysteries in human history. Study guide included. *978-0-8308-3435-8, DVD*

Evil and the Justice of God
N. T. Wright explores all aspects of evil and how it presents itself in society today. Fully grounded in the story of the Old and New Testaments, this presentation is provocative and hopeful; a fascinating analysis of and response to the fundamental question of evil and justice that faces believers. *978-0-8308-3398-6, 176 pages, hardcover*

Evil
Filmed in Israel, South Africa and England, this 50-minute DVD confronts some of the major "evil" issues of our time—from tsunamis to AIDS—and puts them under the biblical spotlight. N. T. Wright says there is a solution to the problem of evil, if only we have the honesty and courage to name it and understand it for what it is. Study guide included. *978-0-8308-3434-1, DVD*

Justification: God's Plan and Paul's Vision
In this comprehensive account and defense of the crucial doctrine of justification, Wright also responds to critics who have challenged what has come to be called the New Perspective. Ultimately, he provides a chance for those in the middle of and on both sides of the debate to interact directly with his views and form their own conclusions. *978-0-8308-3863-9, 279 pages, hardcover*

Small Faith—Great God
N. T. Wright reminds us that what matters is not how much faith we have but Who our faith is in. Wright looks at the character of the faith God calls us to. He unfolds how dependence, humility and mystery all have a role to play. But the author doesn't ignore the messiness and difficulties of life, when hard times come and the unexpected knocks us down. He opens to us what faith means in times of trial and even in the face of death. Through it all he reminds us, it's

not great faith we need: it is faith in a great God. *978-0-8308-3833-2, 176 pages, hardcover*

Colossians and Philemon
In Colossians, Paul presents Christ as "the firstborn over all creation," and appeals to his readers to seek a maturity found only Christ. In Philemon, Paul appeals to a fellow believer to receive a runaway slave in love and forgiveness. In this volume N. T. Wright offers comment on both of these important books. *978-0-8308-4242-1, 199 pages, paperback*